BERLITZ

# MALTA

- A ✓ in the text denotes a highly recommended sight
- A complete A–Z of practical information starts on p.105
- Extensive mapping on cover flaps

Printed in Switzerland by Weber SA, Bienne.

1st edition (1993/4)

**Although we make every effort to ensure the accuracy of the information in this guide, changes do occur. If you have any new information, suggestions or corrections to contribute, we would like to hear from you. Please write to Berlitz Publishing at the above address.**

| | |
|---|---|
| Text: | Martin Gostelow |
| Editors: | Jane Middleton, Sarah Hudson |
| Photography: | Martin Gostelow |
| Thanks to: | Air Malta, the Malta National Tourism Organization, Connie Grech, Leslie Agius, Mario Falzon, Joseph Abela and Avis Malta for their invaluable help in the preparation of this guide. |
| Cartography: | Falk-Verlag, Hamburg |

Front cover photograph: © Telegraph Colour Library

## CONTENTS

# The Islands and the People

The strategic position of Malta, Gozo and Comino has made these Mediterranean islands a crossroads of history and often a bone of contention. Less than 100km (60 miles) south of Sicily and 350km (220 miles) north of the deserts of Libya, they are now easily accessible to today's jet-age travellers. Reliable summers and warm seas make them a great place for a beach holiday, with the added attractions of dozens of sights and monuments from a fascinating past.

Approached by air or sea, Malta can look arid and austere, especially when baked by a midday sun. But as you get nearer, the landscape of the main island takes on a special beauty. The pastel colours of the rocks are networked with dry stone walls, trapping pockets of greenery. Here and there a surprisingly large or opulent church will stand out from an almost biblical village scene of flat-topped houses. In cobalt-blue harbours and narrow inlets, the multi-coloured *luzzu* fishing boats bob alongside yachts, cruise ships and mammoth oil tankers.

Once on the ground, you'll find a land full of contrasts. In winter, even the most barren-looking rock sparkles with tiny wild narcissus and crocuses. And when spring arrives, the hills blaze with colour. Horse-drawn carts vie for road space with big new cars and middle-aged collectors' pieces from the fifties, lovingly kept going by ingenious mechanics. They drive on the left in Malta, and if you were to judge only from that and the bright red post and telephone boxes, you could believe you were in England.

Valletta, the capital city, is ringed by massive bastions. Built originally for defence, their architecture is admired by visitors from all over the world; for one of Malta's biggest industries these days is tourism. Hotels line the bays and rocky shores north and west of Valletta, and for most of the year the islands bask in sunshine. In summer the temperature can soar, but wherever you are, the temptingly clear blue Mediterranean is never far away and always ready to refresh. Winter visitors have increased in number year by year, fleeing the cold of northern Europe and attracted by lower off-season prices.

The main island of Malta covers just 246sq km (95sq miles), one sixth the size of Greater London, and you can travel around easily from place to place by car, bus or taxi. Gozo is even smaller, at 67sq km (26sq miles). Reached only by boat or perhaps by helicopter, it stays just the way its

*Many 1950's cars are still going, thanks to loving owners and ingenious mechanics. Take a drive past sparkling wild crocuses.*

inhabitants and visitors like it – a rural outpost. Between Malta and Gozo, tiny Comino is about 2.7sq km (1sq mile) in area, has one hotel, a handful of permanent residents and no cars.

The total population of the island nation is estimated to be about 357,000, of whom about one in ten lives on Gozo. The first inhabitants arrived in the islands during Neolithic times, around 7,000 years ago. Colonized by almost every Mediterranean power from Phoenicians to the Knights of the Order of St John, and latterly the British, the country finally became an independent nation in 1964.

From these differing roots, the Maltese have emerged. For the most part they are sturdy and dark haired, almost all great swimmers and good sailors. Visitors are invariably impressed by the islanders, who are among the most polite and good-natured people in the world. They are proud but also fun-loving, and know how to laugh at themselves as well as with everyone else. Work gets

done – even back-breaking toil if necessary – but it is not taken too seriously.

Everyone speaks the Maltese language, *Malti*, which is much more akin to Arabic than anything else (the numbers sound almost exactly the same in both). That surely represents a remarkable survival. It is nearly 900 years since Arab rule was ended by the Norman invasion from Sicily, and since then various occupying powers have used strong pressure to get the people to use their language, whether it be Spanish, French, Italian or English. Not surprisingly, words from each of the above did get incorporated, but generally *Malti* seems inaccessible to foreigners. You'll pick up a few words from signs, as many street names are in *Malti* now. The word for street is *triq* – but the 'q' is almost silent. Some of the other consonants are pronounced in apparently exotic ways, but it's worth knowing the rules so that you can say place names correctly. *Xewkija* on Gozo, for example, is pronounced 'shoo-KEE-yah' (see also LANGUAGE on p.117).

English-speaking tourists have few problems on Malta, as English is taught in schools and almost all Maltese speak it well. Italian too is widely understood, and not only for historical reasons – it was the official language of the knights – and the proximity of Italy. Today, many of Italy's television channels that broadcast from Sicily are picked up by forests of tall antennae in Malta, and the young generation is growing up with Italian children's programmes, pop music and sport.

Malta became Christian after St Paul was shipwrecked there in AD 60. Today, you can visit the cave where the apostle is believed to have spent that winter. Religion is taken seriously, and there are magnificent churches, wayside chapels and shrines everywhere. Each parish is fiercely proud of its church – here, keeping up with the Joneses means giving your church more expensive ornaments and decoration. Taken to the limit, it means raising a great deal of money and building a bigger one.

The loud bangs you hear on weekdays probably come from the huge quarries where they dig out the stone for the rapid building programme. But during weekends in summer, other explosions mark a succession of religious festivities or *festi*. Each town and village celebrates its saint's day with parades, brass bands and fireworks. The churches bring out their precious relics and their best silver and damask hangings. Streets and squares are decorated with huge statues of saints and special lighting, and they throng with people. Holy masses are said and sung, but

*Horse-drawn carriages wait to take you on a grand tour of the narrow streets of Mdina.*

there's also the atmosphere of a country fair.

Malta has produced many good artists, though some of the finest paintings you'll see in the cathedrals, churches and museums were done by the Italian painters Michelangelo Caravaggio and Mattia Preti. The chances are, however, that the building housing them was the work of one of the brilliant Maltese architects, such as Gerolamo Cassar or Lorenzo Gafà. Their designs and the warm local stone add up to a special look, unique to Malta.

The stone-carvers who embellished baroque palaces with statues have modern counterparts. Look out for the graceful and dynamic figures of the 20th-century sculptor Antonio Sciortino which can be found in museums and other public places. And although the local artisans' work today can be repetitive, you'll still find beautiful and original designs in blown and moulded glass, silver filigree, lace and pottery.

The Maltese islands are far from being entirely given over to leisure facilities and the production of souvenirs. Part of their attraction is the way life goes on largely unaffected by tourism. Even the resort areas are a major part of the local scene. Farming, fishing, light industry (brewing, printing, canning and textiles) and Valletta's colossal dry docks and other ship-repair facilities are big employers. Even so, there have often been hard times and not enough work – many Maltese emigrated in large numbers to Australia, Canada and the United States. Those who prospered overseas were able to realize a dream – to come home. All over Malta and Gozo you'll see houses with names like 'Sydney', or 'God Bless America'.

The islands are full of fun and surprises round every corner: children playing with a pet goat; an old woman clicking her bobbins to produce spiderwebs of lace; a *karrozzin* (a real 'surrey with a fringe on top'). There's mystery too, as you wander through the prehistoric ruins of some of the oldest temples on earth at Ħaġar Qim (see p.73) or Ġgantija (see p.81). Nobody can fully explain the strange lost civilizations that built them.

You won't need anyone to help you enjoy the pleasures of the seashore, the little sandy beaches, swimming off the rocks and the myriad watersports. Whatever your interests – archaeological, artistic, religious or sporting – you'll find something to satisfy you on Malta, with the prospect of time to relax by the pool or a well-deserved leisurely lunch after your exertions.

*Geometrical perfection is displayed in a fish trap fashioned by a Gozo craftsman.*

# A Brief History

Often ruled but never truly dominated, the Maltese islands command a place in history to match their strategic location. Over the centuries, each nation with power and ambitions in the Mediterranean has eyed them covetously. Violence, intrigue and courage mark the many battles fought for their possession. Malta has been called 'a palimpsest of history' – meaning an original manuscript erased and written over many times.

Civilization dawned on the islands long before recorded history. Fishermen setting sail from Sicily were probably the first to spot the islands, and in about 5000 BC (for a comment on prehistoric dates, see p.62) the first settlers arrived. They were Stone Age farmers, who lived in caves and villages and made simple pottery. A religious cult of the dead evolved – or was introduced – and became highly organized, to judge by the quite complex architecture of the time.

You can visit many of the prehistoric sites. One extraordinary underground complex of cave-like tombs on Malta is at Paola (see p.75). Known as the Hypogeum, it was in use from about 3200 to 2500 BC, towards the end of the Stone Age in the islands. Its elliptical-shaped rooms and passages both served as a burial chamber, and perhaps also a temple. The basic architectural forms found here also appear in such enormous stone temples as Ġgantija on Gozo and Ħaġar Qim on Malta.

Some of the most magnificent prehistoric buildings were the temples of the Tarxien period (about 3200-2500 BC), named after the place where several of them are located. These are a stunning feat of construction for a supposedly primitive society. After them, the building of temples came to a sudden end, possibly as a result of invasion, though other theories suggest a plague or the pressures of over-population.

A new wave of immigrants appears to have come from southern Italy. Known as the

'Cemetery People', they used the Tarxien temples as a burial ground but left only fragmentary traces of their culture. Far more relics have survived from the era of their Bronze Age successors, who built fortified villages – including Borġ in-Nadur, where the defensive wall dating from 1500 BC is still visible.

*The megalithic temples of Tarxien lay buried for thousands of years until rediscovered in 1913.*

## Carthage and Rome

By the 9th century BC, Phoenician sailors from the eastern Mediterranean had reached the Maltese islands. At about the same time, they established a colony at Carthage in North Africa which grew into a great trading republic, eclipsing the Phoenician cities of the east and dominating the whole region. Inscriptions, coins and tombs remain as a record of their control in Malta.

### The Great 'Cart Track' Mystery

Some of the stoniest ground found in Malta and Gozo is criss-crossed with prehistoric 'cart tracks'.

These ruts have been discovered near village sites and quarries, and although they are not always of the same width and were probably nothing to do with wheeled carts at all, they seem to have been made by vehicles of some kind. These were probably 'slide carts', with two shafts attached to a draught animal and dragging two stones linked by a crossbar. The load of building material or produce would have been carried on the bar.

Among the best places to see cart tracks are near Dingli, the so-called 'Clapham Junction' site (see p.54), and Ta' Ċenċ on Gozo (see p.84).

Greek civilization was another strong influence. The Greeks do not seem to have settled on Malta, but they had colonies in nearby Sicily and there was frequent contact.

When a new power, Rome, began to expand southwards, the clash with Carthage was inevitable. During the three Punic Wars between these two powers, from 264 to 146 BC, the Carthaginians were forced to give up their Empire and were finally defeated. Malta was taken by a Roman expedition in 218 BC under the command of the consul Tiberius Sempronius.

The Carthaginians had built their capital up on the hilltop where Mdina now stands, and the Romans took this over, fortifying it and building luxurious villas. You can see the remains of a Roman house between Mdina and Rabat.

One of Malta's most important historical events occurred during the Romans' rule. In AD 60, St Paul along with St Luke, were shipwrecked on the island, somewhere in the area now known as St Paul's Bay.

Paul's preaching in Jerusalem and Caesarea had caused such an outcry among the religious leaders there that the Romans had arrested him, partly for his own safety. During the subsequent enquiry Paul claimed the right, as a Roman citizen, to appeal to Caesar for justice. It was while he and Luke were travelling from Caesarea to Rome, as prisoners, that their ship foundered on the rocky coast of Malta in a storm.

For a whole winter they stayed in a cave at Mdina-Rabat, and St Paul preached the gospel. His message and the miracles that were reported to have happened in his presence began the conversion of the islanders to Christianity. Even the Roman governor, Publius, became a convert, and

*The fine, intricate mosaic floor from the Roman villa at Rabat, near the Mdina Gate.*

eventually he became the first Bishop of Malta. He was later martyred and canonized. Despite the many changes since then, including a period of Moslem rule, Malta has remained fundamentally Christian from St Paul's time to the present day.

**What's in a Name?**

The origin of Malta's name has often been debated. The most plausible theories are that it is either a corruption of the Phoenician *malat* (meaning 'safe harbour'), or that it comes from the Greek *meli* (the word for 'honey'), a famous product of the islands in early times.

Gozo (or Għawdex, pronounced 'Ow-dehsh') is probably derived from the Greek *gaudos,* which in turn comes from the Phoenician for a small boat.

## Arabs and Crusaders

As the Roman Empire went into decline, it was divided into western and eastern sections, and Malta was allocated to the east, governed from Constantinople. In AD 870, the Arabs became the new rulers.

Although Christianity was tolerated, it seems that many islanders emigrated, and some became Moslems. At that time slave trade was big business, pursued by both Arabs and the Maltese. The victims were mainly Christians who were captured either at sea or in raids on neighbouring coasts.

Two centuries of Arab rule left an indelible impression on Malta and especially on the language (see p.7). Cotton and citrus fruits were grown and became the mainstay of the economy as Malta's trade expanded.

However, quarrels amongst the Arabs eventually weakened the islands' defences, and the Norman Count Roger, son of Tancred de Hauteville, seized his chance. Roger had inherited lands in southern Italy and Sicily and wanted to improve his strategic position by controlling Malta. He came ashore at St Paul's Bay in 1090, later

taking Mdina and the rest of the islands, which became part of the Kingdom of Sicily.

The new ruler was fairly liberal, letting the islanders govern themselves with local councils. The Christian church was encouraged to expand and renew itself, although Moslems were tolerated. Malta became a key link in the line of communication during the Crusades, while passing first into the hands of the Swabians and then to Charles of Anjou, brother of the French king, Louis IX. The French stayed until they were ousted in 1283 by Peter I of Aragon.

Exploitation by overseas feudal lords, interested in the country mainly as a source of revenue, continued under joint Spanish-Sicilian control. The Maltese worked at commerce, farming and slave-trading, as

*The walled city of Mdina was the capital of Malta under Carthaginian, Roman and Arab rule.*

well as piracy, in order to earn the taxes demanded of them.

By the 15th century, local self-government had evolved into an administrative body called the Università. Weary with having to pay extortionate dues to foreign nobles, the Maltese people raised money to secure instead a direct relationship with Spain. In 1428, King Alfonso V declared it 'reunited in perpetuity' to the crown, cutting out the landlords. However, the islanders' problems were not over. There were repeated attacks by Turkish raiders and pirates from North Africa. By the 16th century, with Spain's attention now drawn to the New World, morale was low and the economy was in decline.

## The Knights of St John

At this time, Suleiman the Magnificent, who was Sultan of the Ottoman Turks, practically ruled the Mediterranean Sea. The Knights of the Order of St John had long since been expelled from the Holy Land but had found a base on the island of Rhodes. Now, after repeated attacks and a six-month siege in 1522, the Turks took Rhodes on New Year's Day 1523 and the knights were adrift again.

Philippe Villiers de l'Isle-Adam, the courageous Grand Master of the Order, led his soldiers to Sicily and Italy. But Europe's loyalties were divided between King Francis I of France and Charles V, Holy Roman Emperor and King of Spain and Sicily.

Finding a more permanent home for the knights was becoming a thorny problem.

After seven years of negotiations, the knights reluctantly agreed to take over Malta in exchange for the payment of one falcon a year (the famous 'Maltese falcon', though not much to do with the film of the same name). In 1530, the Grand Master and his 4,000 men moved to the new base.

The islanders were naturally uneasy about these new-

**The Knights of St John**

The story of the Order of the Hospital of St John of Jerusalem (the Knights Hospitallers) begins in the 11th century, when several Italian merchants obtained permission from the Moslem *caliph* to set up a hospice in Jerusalem for Christian pilgrims. The calling of the brothers of the Order was principally to care for the sick, but in time the emphasis shifted to a military role, that of fighting for the faith.

In 1187 the knights were driven from Jerusalem by Saladin and had to move to Acre and then on to Cyprus. They retreated further, to Rhodes, in 1308, and though the Turks also besieged that island several times, it wasn't until 1522 that the power of Suleiman the Magnificent forced them to surrender and move on yet again.

The brothers took vows of poverty, chastity and obedience. They were divided into three main grades: Knights of Justice (from noble families all over Europe, who wore the eight-pointed cross now known as the Maltese cross), Sergeants at Arms (who acted as both soldiers and nurses), and Chaplains (who worked in the hospitals and churches).

comers at first, but their rights were properly respected and many appreciated the presence of these powerful protectors.

The knights set about building fortifications and living quarters in Birgu (later called Vittoriosa) and the neighbouring peninsula, Senglea. As the Grand Harbour area became the focus of activity, so the importance of the old capital, Mdina, was correspondingly reduced.

Grand Master Villiers de l'Isle-Adam died in 1534 and was succeeded by several other Grand Masters. Then in 1557 the leadership passed to one whose name was to become famous in Malta's history, Jean Parisot de la Valette.

Soon after the knights arrived in Malta, the Turks began

The knights were grouped in eight *langues* or 'tongues', three of them French (France being divided in the 13th century into France, Provence and Auvergne). The other *langues* were Aragon, Castile, Italy, Germany and England. After the Reformation the English *langue* ceased to exist, though a new joint *langue* of England and Bavaria was formed in 1784. Each *langue* was headed by a *pilier*, who had a set function: thus the *pilier* of Italy was Grand Admiral; the *pilier* of Provence was finance and ordnance manager; the *pilier* of France was head of the Order's hospitals.

In the 16th century, the knights had over 650 *commanderies* and huge estates all over Europe. Their head, the Grand Master, was elected for life and was subject only to the authority of the Pope.

As the years passed, the knights lapsed into careless and even dissolute ways. Corruption and internal dissension undermined the effectiveness and reputation of the Order. Some of the original ideals of the Hospitallers are continued in the St John Ambulance Association: the Order itself, now based in Rome, does mainly charitable work.

to attack them again, with an eye to taking the island because of its strategic position on Mediterranean sea routes.

The North African 'Barbary' pirates, under command of their leader, Dragut, were another threat. They devastated the island of Gozo in 1546 and took thousands of Gozitans as slaves in 1551. When Dragut then joined forces with the Turks, the future for Christendom looked bleak.

## The Great Siege

Suleiman the Magnificent decided the time was ripe for new Islamic victories, so he began an unprecedented build-up of warships and troops. Word reached Grand Master de la Valette, and he sent out desperate appeals for help, but only a few volunteers came. On 19 May 1565, a Turkish fleet of 138 galleys disembarked an army of 38,000 at Marsaxlokk

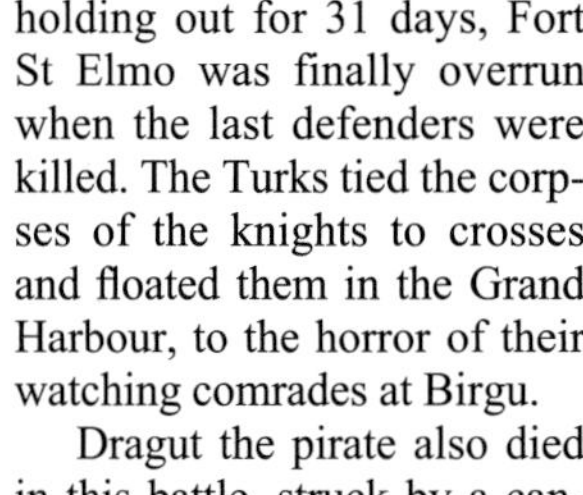

Bay. Among them were 4,000 of the fanatical, feared janissaries, many of them converts to Islam and all trained only for war.

The invaders, commanded by Admiral Piali and Mustapha Pasha, were confident of victory. De la Valette had only his 600 knights, 9,000 other troops and eight galleys, but they conducted one of the most valiant defences in history. It was punctuated by disasters. After holding out for 31 days, Fort St Elmo was finally overrun when the last defenders were killed. The Turks tied the corpses of the knights to crosses and floated them in the Grand Harbour, to the horror of their watching comrades at Birgu.

Dragut the pirate also died in this battle, struck by a cannonball, thus depriving the attackers of one of their most determined leaders. The spot where he fell, on Marsamxett Harbour, is now known as Dragut Point.

De la Valette strengthened his defences at Senglea and Birgu, and linked the two by a bridge of boats so that reinforcements could be rushed from one to the other. The crisis was at hand and all of Christian Europe seemed to hold its breath – but still sent no help. Word even reached Protestant England, where the Queen, Elizabeth I, ordered

*Fort St Angelo, Vittoriosa, was the knights' command post during the Great Siege.*

prayers to be said in all the churches of her realm.

Throughout the terrible summer of 1565, heat, disease and dwindling food supplies plagued both sides as they battled on. The Maltese people fought and suffered along with the knights in fierce resistance.

Despite their superior numbers, their explosives and their dedication, the Turks were slowly worn down. Arguments between their commanders did not help. In one assault on Senglea, the Turks lost 2,500 men. Though the knights' losses were fewer, they were more serious because irreplaceable, and strategic positions were abandoned one by one for lack of troops to hold them. At one critical point for the knights, even de la Valette himself (though he was 72) threw himself into the fray, inspiring his followers by his courage.

At last reinforcements for the beseiged were mustered by the Sicilian Viceroy, Garcia de Toledo, and on 7 September, they landed at Mellieha Bay. The Turks were running out of supplies, leadership and spirit: fooled into believing the fresh troops to be more numerous than they really were, they lifted the siege. The remnant of their forces sailed away: historians estimate that well over two-thirds had been lost. There followed general rejoicing in Malta, though the main island was devastated.

In the aftermath there was fierce debate about reconstruction and new fortifications: the cost was clearly beyond the knights' resources. Some even suggested moving yet again to another base, but in the event the European powers proved more generous with money than they had been with help during the siege. Plans were drawn up for a new city between the two long harbours, on the Sceberras peninsula. The Order obtained the services of the Pope's own architect, Laparelli. Named after the dauntless de la Valette, Valletta, the capital, was born (the double L results from the Italian version of his name).

During the two centuries of the knights' rule that followed, Malta's trade at first prospered and there was a building boom. Laparelli was succeeded by the Maltese architect, Gerolamo Cassar, who was responsible for much of the way Valletta looks today: harmonious styles blending early baroque with classical.

By the 18th century, Mediterranean traders were feeling the effects of the alternative route to the riches of the East, round the Cape of Good Hope, and the new magnet of the Americas. With their old enemies the Ottoman Turks no longer a threat, the Order too was declining into a dissolute middle age. The French Revolution of 1789, and the subsequent downfall of the aristocracy and the church in France, deprived the knights of much of their support – and most of their revenue.

## Enter Napoleon

In 1798, with mastery of the Mediterranean his objective, Napoleon came to the same conclusion as many commanders before and since: Malta would be valuable to him, and would pose a threat if held by his enemies. On 10 June he invaded the island, landing at Valletta, where he presented the knights with an order: they must pack up and leave. Where others had failed, Napoleon succeeded. Grand Master de Hompesch gave in, and, after 268 years of residence, the world's most famous military Order departed.

Napoleon started energetically promulgating new laws, but then he too left, only six days after the knights. Two years of French rule followed, in which the arrogant behaviour of the occupiers made them hated by both the Maltese and the Church. A popular insurrection began, and lasted on and off for 18 months until troops sent by the King of Naples joined the Maltese.

With Admiral Nelson patrolling the Mediterranean, the French position was hopeless, and they capitulated in 1800. In 1802 the Treaty of Amiens gave Malta back to the Order of St John, but subsequent Maltese protests prevented the knights from returning.

*The inland towns of Malta (below is Attard) seem to bask, half asleep, in the afternoon sun.*

Malta's value as a naval base now came to the attention of the British, who had just relinquished Menorca. For the remainder of the Napoleonic Wars, Great Britain informally

administered the islands, and her possession was formally recognized in the Treaty of Paris in 1814, and again at the Congress of Vienna. British rule was to last until 1964, and her forces continued to use bases on Malta until 1979.

## British Colony

In the early years, the British set about imposing some sort of uniformity with the rest of their growing Empire. In 1813, a year marked by a plague which killed off a fifth of its people, Sir Thomas Maitland arrived as governor of Malta. Nicknamed 'King Tom', he dismissed the traditional self-governing Università and introduced sweeping reforms to bring the legal system into line with the English one – though old practices often persisted.

With this degree of stability and improving health standards, the population grew considerably, though the economy had its ups and downs. New crops were introduced, including potatoes, which all flourished. Water resources were better managed and more vineyards were planted. Cotton production, once all-important, declined in the face of large-scale competition from Egypt and America, and attempts to start a silk industry failed.

The building of bases for the Royal Navy, plus a harbour and ship-repair facilities gave a boost to employment and prosperity. The opening of the Suez Canal in 1869 increased Mediterranean shipping and by 1880, Grand Harbour was a major port. Later, many rivals developed, with greater home markets and industries, thus diminishing Malta's importance as a centre of trade.

During the 19th century, a succession of constitutions gave Malta varying degrees of autonomy. In a world of falling Empires and revolutions after the First World War, local riots in 1919 brought about real changes, codified in the new Constitution of 1921. The Maltese became responsible for their own internal affairs although London, through the British Governor, retained control of both defence and foreign affairs, and any matters affecting the Empire and further political turmoil led to the constitution being suspended more than once in the years that followed.

## The Second Great Siege

During World War II, Malta was vital to the Allied cause. Not only could ships and aircraft based there block the deployment of Italy's navy, they could also attack Axis supply routes to the German and Italian forces operating from North Africa (notably Rommel's Afrika Korps). It was therefore inevitable that the same Axis powers should attempt to eliminate the threat that Malta posed. When Italy entered the war in June 1940, its first move was to bomb Malta and, during 1941, Italian and later German bombers and fighters, based on Sicily and mainland Italy, kept up almost incessant raids.

As Rommel made his advance through Egypt in spring 1942, enemy air attacks increased, and in March and April the islands were hit with more than twice the weight of bombs that fell on London during any *year* of the war. That summer, life came close to being unbearable on Malta, with people living in cellars and caves in conditions of near-starvation.

The war cabinet in London decided to take the huge risk of trying to force a way through to the beleaguered islands by sending a major convoy carrying desperately needed supplies. This perilous operation was code-named *Pedestal.* In August 1942, 13 supply ships and a tanker made their way, with both naval and air cover, through the straits of Gibraltar. In a succession of Italian air attacks on the convoy, several of its ships were sunk and the tanker *Ohio*, with its precious oil, was badly damaged. However, four cargo ships reached Valletta and on 15 August, despite five days of fierce bombardment, the *Ohio* was towed into Grand Harbour to a reception of weeping and cheering crowds: Malta had been resupplied and would fight on.

By November, with Allied landings in Morocco and Rommel's forces in retreat from Egypt after the battle of El Alamein, Malta began to see the promise of victory that its own courage and sacrifice had made possible.

The price of freedom had been high. Thousands of men, women and children had been killed or injured and thousands of homes destroyed. It was only fitting, concluded Churchill, that Malta be awarded Britain's highest honour for civilian courage – the George Cross. To this day, it appears on the national flag.

## Independence

After the war, Britain gave Malta financial assistance with plans for reconstruction, and a new constitution granted them self-government within the Commonwealth. Plans for the complete transfer of power met with difficulties in both Malta and the United Kingdom, but, on 21 September 1964, Malta became fully independent with a Governor-General and a Parliament of 50 members (now 65). In 1971 the Labour Party was voted in with Dom Mintoff as Prime Minister.

British forces remained on some military bases, but they finally left on 1 April 1979. Their withdrawal brought an end to the friction between Britain and the Mintoff government, but also saw the end of British financial aid, and thus the beginning of unemployment among those who had depended on the British services for their livelihoods.

There was some sadness on both sides at the parting of the ways. Maltese pride in independence did not lessen their goodwill towards British residents on Malta and Gozo and the thousands of Britons who spend their holidays there.

The years since independence have seen the government change hands between the evenly balanced Nationalist and Labour parties. Malta's accounced aim to join the European Community will not in any way conflict with the ever-increasing self-confidence of a free nation.

# Where to Go

In this chapter we start with Valletta and the suburbs, move on to Mdina and Rabat and then visit the south-east coast and the north west. The special section on Malta's prehistoric temples gathers together the information on these ancient and mysterious cultures for handy reference. Finally, we give a complete summary of where to go on Gozo.

But first, the city that has been at the centre of Malta's turbulent history ...

# Valletta

'That splendid town, quite like a dream', wrote Sir Walter Scott. When you see Valletta, whether from the air, or from a boat, or in the glow of the late afternoon sun, you'll agree with him. The light turns the city's bright stone bastions and buildings to gold, making it a place of enchantment which seems to float on an indigo sea.

It was not always this way. Mdina, the walled inland city, was the capital of Malta from pre-Roman times until the Great Siege of 1565. But the Grand Master, Jean Parisot de la Valette, saw the defensive possibilities of the Sceberras peninsula and his imagination was fired. After the knights' victory, plans were laid to build a capital there, with invulnerable fortifications. The sharply hog-backed ridge with its two great natural harbours, Marsamxett on one side and the Grand Harbour on the other, was the perfect place. So it was that in 1566, despite the enormous cost anticipated, work was begun by Francesco Laparelli, who had served as architect to Cosimo de' Medici and Pope Pius IV.

*Contrasts abound in Grand Harbour: a traditional* luzzu *and a supertanker in for repairs.*

Laparelli is said to have masterminded the entire city plan in a mere three days, and two years later, when he left, Gerolamo Cassar (his Maltese assistant) took over and kept to the original conception.

The new city was constructed quickly but intelligently. Around the uniform grid-shaped street plan, a solid line of stone curtains and bastions was built, which made it virtually impregnable.

Fresh water remained a problem until the 17th century, when Grand Master Alof de Wignacourt ordered the construction of an aqueduct from springs near Mdina: this new supply even allowed gardens to be added near to the fortifications.

Valletta suffered merciless bombing during World War II, but it was a victorious and courageous Maltese people who wept with joy when the blockade was broken in 1942 (see also p.26). They are proud of their city, and have kept its original charms intact.

**Fortifications Galore**

In the 16th century, any new city required fortifications of one kind or another. Valletta, Floriana and their surrounding suburbs can boast enough bastions, curtains, forts, towers, cavaliers, ravelins, ramparts, trenches, ditches, walls and other defensive structures to send any budding military engineer into frissons of ecstasy.

The typical zig-zag bastion provided the most effective type of defence. The nearer the enemy approached the bastion, the easier it became for the defenders to fire on the attackers along the flanks. Defences were thus 'strengthened' without a real increase in arms, ammunition or men.

The best way to appreciate Valletta's fortifications (most of which date from 1566-70) is to walk along the tops of them. To go round completely takes about two hours (allowing time for stopping to admire the views).

## AROUND THE OLD TOWN

The best way to visit Valletta is on foot. Driving is inadvisable, as the streets are narrow and many are closed to traffic. Sunset is a good time for a walk round, when the shadows are cooling the streets, and you can join strollers out for the evening social hour known as the *passeggiata*.

From the roundabout bus terminal and Triton Fountain, a footbridge crosses the deep rock-cut defensive ditch. You pass through the City Gate – rebuilt in postwar style – and into Freedom Square, with an arcade and complex of shops on either side. Directly ahead is Republic Street, which is closed to motor traffic for most of the day. Parallel to it on the right is the second principal

*The Auberge de Castile et Léon, now the PMs office, was originally designed by Cassar.*

*An evocation of times past, a bust of Sir Winston Churchill takes pride of place in the delightful Upper Barrakka Gardens.*

artery, Merchants Street. Both streets run on for 1.5km (almost 1 mile) to Fort St Elmo at the end of the peninsula.

Opposite City Gate you'll see sad ruins of the classical old opera house built by E.M. Barry – a reminder of the bombing in World War II. To the right is Valletta's oldest church, the baroque **Our Lady of Victories**, completed in 1567 as a commemoration of the Great Siege victory (its front was remodelled in the 17th century). Next to it a crumbling reddish façade is what remains of one of the earliest houses built in the city. Opposite is the church of St Catherine of Italy, a domed structure originally designed by Cassar, but later rebuilt.

A few steps further on is the **Auberge de Castile et Léon**, most impressive of the *auberges*, now housing the office of the Prime Minister. The *auberges* (inns) are the buildings where the knights were accommodated. Each *langue* had its own *auberge*. Unfortunately the public can see it from the outside only.

Just beyond Castile Place are the **Upper Barrakka Gardens**, built in the 18th century. With green shrubs and trees, bright hibiscus and statues, the area is a pleasant retreat where the knights used to stroll and supposedly hatch plots, or where the people watched them set off on expeditions. Among the statues you'll see today are a group of children, *Les Gavroches*, by Antonio Sciortino, the Maltese sculptor; a monument to Lord Strickland, Prime Minister from 1927-30; a bust of Sir Winston Churchill; and the tomb of Sir Thomas Maitland, 'King Tom', the peppery governor of Malta (and Corfu) from 1813-24 (see also p.25).

From under the colonnade here there's a stunning **view** across Grand Harbour. On the far left guarding the harbour mouth is the 17th-century Fort Ricasoli; directly ahead is Fort St Angelo (Grand Master de la Valette's headquarters in the Great Siege) at Vittoriosa; to the right is Dockyard Creek, where the knights had their boats repaired. The next promontory is Senglea (see p. 45), behind which rises the town of Cospicua, built later when the defensive walls were extended by Grand Master Cotoner. Directly below you, on Lascaris Wharf, is the old Customs House, attractively built in Venetian style, and several well-restored warehouses.

Return to Merchants Street and youll see **Parisio Palace**, on the right, where Napoleon stayed for a few days in 1798. Now the Ministry of Foreign Affairs, the palace is a sober 18th-century building. On the opposite side of the street the Auberge d'Italie, built by Cassar in the 16th century, was later modified and is now the General Post Office.

Make your way from Merchants Street to **Republic Street** via Melita Street. This thoroughfare is a hive of activity, lined with all kinds of shops, cafés and snack bars. The **Church of Santa Barbara** (between South Street and Melita Street) is unusual for its simple decoration and oval shape beneath a soaring dome. This church was used by the knights of the *langue* of Provence. Today the Catholic services are held here in English, French and German.

Conveniently nearby, the **Auberge de Provence**, on your left as you head towards Fort St Elmo, now houses the

**National Museum of Archaeology** (for opening hours, see p.122). This *auberge*, founded in 1571, was designed by Gerolamo Cassar.

The museum's collection, begun in the 17th and 18th centuries and reorganized in the 20th century by the Maltese archaeologist, Sir Themistocles Zammit, was brought here when the museum was inaugurated in 1957.

It's essential to see this collection for a better understanding of Malta's prehistoric sites. Among the fascinating objects here are the celebrated 13cm- (5in-) long 'Sleeping Woman' statuette from the Hypogeum underground burial chambers, and the huge lower half of a 'fat lady' transplanted from Tarxien, where she was being eroded by the elements. Stones showing the early 'pitted' style of decoration or the later spiral form have been brought here from Ħaġar Qim, Tarxien and other sites (and replaced there by replicas) for the same reason.

There are also artefacts from each of Malta's prehistoric periods – such as carbonized seeds and weapons, and a curious Tarxien plate engraved with bulls and goats. The shards of big bowls and vases from the Tarxien period have since been reassembled, and from the number found, it is thought that breaking vessels may have been part of the ancient religious cult.

Upstairs, the museum has some interesting Roman and Punic (Carthaginian) pottery and jewellery, and a *cippus* (small pillar) with inscriptions in both Phoenician and Greek, which enabled scholars to find the key to the deciphering of Phoenician. Its twin was given to Louis XIV and is now in the Louvre in Paris.

After leaving the museum, if you turn again towards Fort St Elmo, you'll see **St John's Square** and the Cathedral just off to the right. A crafts centre is housed in a corner of the square, and the neighbouring section of Merchants Street becomes a delightful open-air market on weekday mornings (on Sundays it moves to St James' Ditch).

**St John's Co-Cathedral** (for opening hours, see p.123), the knights' own church, was built between 1573-77 to the plans of Gerolamo Cassar. It is considered to be his masterpiece and was raised to its cathedral status in 1816 by Pope Pius VII, sharing the distinction with Mdina Cathedral (hence the 'Co-').

The building's rather plain façade does nothing to prepare you for an interior that reveals a quite staggering display of baroque art. Sir Walter Scott wrote that he had never seen a more striking church nave. The barrel-vaulted space is 58m (189ft) long, 20m (64ft) high, and 35m (115ft) wide, and flanked on both sides by **chapels**, most of which were built by the various *langues* of the knights and named after saints. Everywhere you look, this church is densely carved in high relief, gilded or richly painted with religious motifs.

To the right of the nave are the chapels of St James, St George, St Sebastian and the Blessed Sacrament. This last has an extraordinary **screen** and **gates** in solid silver, which, legend has it, were cleverly concealed by being painted black when the French were on a pillaging spree during their occupation of 1798.

The vault of the church is decorated with oil-on-stone **paintings** by the 17th-century Calabrian artist Mattia Preti. They tell the story of St John the Baptist, and took five years (1662-67) to complete.

The rich **high altar** (1681) was designed by the architect Lorenzo Gafà, and presents an elaborate array of marble, silver plate and lapis lazuli. The group behind the altar is of the Baptism of Christ, by Sicilian sculptor Giuseppe Mazzuoli.

The **crypt**, entered from the Chapel of Provence, may be viewed through its gate, and visited on request between 10am and noon; it contains the tombs of the first 12 Grand Masters of Malta.

Going back towards the main door you'll see on the right the chapels of St Charles (or of the Holy Relics), St Michael, St Paul, St Catherine and the Chapel of the Magi. Most chapels have busts or other monuments commemorating Grand Masters. In the sacristy are paintings by Stefano Pieri, Preti and Antoine de Favray.

To reach the **oratory and museum**, take a door on the right facing the altar, third bay from the entrance. The oratory's main feature is the monumental painting by Caravaggio, *The Beheading of St John*, widely considered to be the finest painting in Malta. Commissioned by the Order to paint several works, the hot-tempered Caravaggio ended up assaulting one of the knights. The details of the story are unclear, but the artist left the island in disgrace in 1608. The painting dramatically uses *chiaroscuro* and lively baroque composition well suited to its violent theme.

Back on Republic Street and continuing towards Fort St Elmo, you'll come to Great Siege Square with its powerful allegorical monument by Sciortino. Opposite are the new Law Courts, an imposing neo-classical building on the former site of the Auberge d'Auvergne, destroyed during World War II.

Republic Street widens into **Republic Square**. Most of it is taken up by a spacious outdoor café and lined with little shops under the shady arcades. At the back of the square, the **National Library**, once the Library of the Order, was constructed in the late 18th cen-

*St John's Co-Cathedral is a stunning treasury of semi-precious stones and painted ceilings.*

tury to house the collection amassed by the knights, and the archives of the Order, which includes documents dating back to the 11th century.

From Palace Square, which adjoins Republic Square, you can go through a big archway into the first courtyard of the **Grand Master's Palace**, now the seat of the House of Representatives. In 1569 the nephew of Grand Master del Monte built here what was probably the first private house in Valletta. Later the knights commissioned Gerolamo Cassar to enlarge it into a palace. Today, some parts of the palace house museums, and some of the state rooms are used for Presidential receptions and other national occasions.

You'll find two cool, green courtyards nestled in the palace grounds, one of them called Neptune Court after its statue. In the other, Prince Alfred's Court, look up to see the **clock** installed by Grand Master Pinto de Fonseca (1741-73), with little figures who strike a gong on the hour.

To visit the palace, take the staircase from Prince Alfred Court. In the council chamber, the meeting place of Malta's Parliaments from 1921-76, you

### The Hospital of the Order

The splendid buildings and halls of the Mediterranean Conference Centre started as the hospital of the knights in 1574.

The knights took in anyone of any faith who was ill, and treated the sick as *seigneurs malades* (sick lords) – with respect and humility. The standard of medical treatment was high and the patients were given good food served on silver dishes. All the knights, from the youngest novices to the Grand Master, served the patients.

The hospital was taken over by the French when they occupied Malta, and also later by the British. During the war, the buildings were badly damaged by bombs.

can sit on one of the heavy bench seats and admire the beautiful Gobelins **tapestries** given to the Order by Grand Master Ramon Perellos in the early 18th century. Called *Les Tentures des Indes*, they represent all kinds of real and fanciful beasts and birds, with exotically clad Indians. The paintings above depict the knights' naval victories.

The grandest of the public rooms is the Hall of St Michael and St George, or the Throne Room, with a beamed ceiling and frieze by Matteo Perez d'Aleccio. This is where the Supreme Council of the Order of St John used to meet. Scenes of the Great Siege fill the walls, and the carved gallery comes from the ship in which Villiers de l'Isle-Adam sailed away from Rhodes in 1523.

The damask-curtained **Hall of Ambassadors,** or the Red Room, features heavy portraits of assorted monarchs: Louis XIV by De Troy, Louis XV by Van Loo, Catherine II of Russia by Levitsky.

The **Armoury**, upstairs from Neptune Court, is notable for its immense collection of suits of mail – especially the one worn by Jean de la Valette – and a gold-inlaid ceremonial suit made for Grand Master Alof de Wignacourt. There is also some captured Turkish arms, including, it's said, the corsair Dragut's sword.

Leaving the palace by the Neptune Court archway, you'll see the Greek Catholic Church on Archbishop Street – unremarkable except for a 12th-century **icon**, called 'Our Lady of Damascus', which was brought by the knights when they came to Malta in 1530: it was well restored in 1966. Just a few steps away is the **Gesù Church**, built between 1592-1600, richly ornate in Italian baroque style.

Go down Merchants Street and you'll find yourself at the **Mediterranean Conference Centre**. The restoration of this former hospital is one of the finest achievements of independent Malta. It was accomplished in only a few months and the impressive international conference hall was opened in 1979.

*The Sunday morning market, held below the city walls, is a big and lively weekly event.*

The centre has six well-equipped conference rooms as well as a huge theatre and the beautiful 161m (525ft) vaulted hall that served as the Great Ward in the old hospital. A must for any visitor coming to Malta for the first time is the 45-minute multiscreen documentary, *The Malta Experience*, shown at the centre several times a day. It's an excellent introduction to the history of the islands. Headphones carry the commentary in six languages.

Star-shaped **Fort St Elmo**, so valiantly defended during the Great Siege – though ultimately lost – occupies the whole of the end of the peninsula. You can enter the main part only if you have permission from police headquarters

– the fort is a police academy now. However, within the fort you can visit the **National War Museum**, reached by a separate entrance (for opening hours see p.123). It contains mostly World War II relics, including *Faith*, one of the four Gladiator biplanes that were Malta's air defence when Italy declared war in 1940. The jeep *Husky* was used by General Eisenhower and later by President Roosevelt during a visit. The George Cross, conferred on Malta and the Maltese in 1942 for their courage under bombardment, is one of the most treasured exhibits.

## OTHER PLACES OF INTEREST

If you head back towards City Gate, Fountain Street brings you to the beginning of Strait Street (also known as the Gut), a narrow lane which still has some of the bars and hangouts that once gave it a reputation among sailors for low life. It was also the only place where the knights were allowed to fight duels. A slightly longer walk follows the fortifications, starting along St Sebastian Street with the English Curtain wall on the right and the rather run-down Auberge of the Bavarian *langue* opposite.

After St Sebastian Bastion and its spectacular view over Marsamxett Harbour, if you turn up Archbishop Street – actually consisting of a flight of steps at this point – you'll reach Independence Square. The **Auberge d'Aragon** here was the first *auberge* built in Valletta in the 16th century, the Doric porch was added at a later date. The building of the neo-classical St Paul's Anglican Cathedral opposite was entirely paid for by the Dowager Queen Adelaide after she visited Malta from 1838-39. St Paul's 60m (200ft) high steeple makes a striking landmark, rivalled by the huge dome of **Carmelite Church** nearby on Old Theatre Street, an enlarged replacement for one bombed during the war.

The **Manoel Theatre**, built in 1731 under the rule of Grand Master Manoel de Vilhena, is a gem, and one of Europe's oldest theatres still in use. It endured a period of decay after the larger opera house was opened, becoming at one time a dosshouse (the homeless could sleep in the theatre's boxes for a penny a night) and then a cheap cinema. Now restored as Malta's National Theatre, its neat, oval shape with tiers of gilded and painted boxes makes a splendid setting for both plays and concerts. (Tours begin at the box office in Old Theatre Street – for times see p.123.)

Across the peninsula are several baroque churches: St Roque and St Ursula (both in St Ursula Street) and **St Paul Shipwrecked** in St Paul Street, an 18th-century church with an ornate 19th-century façade. Its treasures include a **statue of St Paul** by Melchiorre Gafà, a wristbone of the saint, and half of the column on which he was beheaded in Rome.

The **National Museum of Fine Arts** is on South Street, which crosses Republic Street up near City Gate. The building is an attractive, white 16th-century palace, built around a sunny courtyard. As Admiralty House, it served as the official residence of the Commander-in-Chief of the British Mediterranean Fleet, a post filled at one time or another by practically every famous British naval hero – as the list inside reminds you.

The collection includes paintings from various periods of the Flemish, Dutch, French and Italian schools, notably some by Mattia Preti, who came to decorate St John's Cathedral and stayed. There are also some fine works by the 20th-century Maltese sculptor Antonio Sciortino.

The exhibits in the basement evoke the knights' hospital mission, with apothecary vessels, vases and the famous **silverware** used to serve the patients. Look out too for the early models of fortifications.

Near City Gate (up to the right before you exit) are **Hastings Gardens**, named after the Marquess of Hastings, who was Governor of Malta from 1824-26. His funerary statue stands here. From here there is a splendid **view** of Marsamxett

Harbour, Msida and Lazzaretto creeks, Manoel Island and Dragut Point. Floriana and St Publius Church are below you and Independence Arena is off to the left.

The mountainous **bastions** of two churches, St Michael and St Andrew, were built up here after the Great Siege and are 18-21m (60-70ft) thick. Walking back to City Gate, before taking a staircase down, you'll cross the fortifications of St James' Cavalier and St John's Cavalier (where the knights now have their Embassy in Malta).

Next to the tourist information office at City Gate, steps lead down into the great 'ditch' that protected Valletta from landward attack. If you make the descent, you'll see the lower-level bridge that once carried Malta's short railway, which went as far as Mdina until it closed in 1931. The station here is now an underground car park.

Along the bottom of the ditch in Lascaris Bastion, the **War Rooms** have been preserved, complete with uniformed models plotting air battles and the progress of convoys (for opening hours see p.123).

# Around Valletta

### FLORIANA

Any approach to Valletta by land inevitably goes through the spacious Floriana area, named after Paolo Floriani, the Italian military engineer who recommended that Valletta be protected by outer fortresses on the land approach.

Here you'll drive under or beside the twin arches of **Porte des Bombes**, one built in the 18th century, another added later, in matching style of course, by the British. On St Anne Street are the British High Commission and the US Embassy.

### VITTORIOSA, SENGLEA, COSPICUA

Just across Grand Harbour from Valletta are 'the three cities', which you can reach by bus from City Gate, by car via

Marsa or, if one is operating, by *dgħajsa* (water taxi) from Lascaris Wharf.

From the main gate of **Vittoriosa**, still known as Birgu to the Maltese, the main street, *Via Il-Mina L-Kbira*, carries on down to Vittoriosa Square. Halfway along you'll come to the former Inquisitor's Palace, a gloomy warren now partly turned into a folk museum. Just to the east of the square in Majjistral (or Mistral) Street is the pretty façade of the **Auberge d'Angleterre**. Below the square, the diminutive church is the Oratory of St Joseph. You can ask for a key at the 'museum' door round the corner – though there's not much to see inside except for a sword and hat belonging to Jean de la Valette.

Towards the waterfront, the **Church of St Lawrence** was originally the knights' Conventual Church before the move to Valletta. It was rebuilt by Lorenzo Gafà in the late 1600s and is richly decorated inside, with paintings and pink marble columns. Outside, a plaque records the death of Sir

### The Harbour by Boat

The two-hour boat tours leaving from Sliema are excellent for a sea view of Valletta and environs. Various companies run the trips several times daily and competition keeps prices down. As you pass container ships and cruise ships, a guide points out the sights – such as the place where the knights put a huge chain across the harbour from St Angelo to Senglea to keep the Turks out – plus the forts and the docks.

In one of the 'creeks', huge tankers are repaired. In another you'll see a dry-dock project built with the help of the People's Republic of China; the 29m (95ft) crane here is one of the world's largest, capable of lifting 150 tonnes. There are more romantic vistas, however, especially of the majestic bastions, spires and domes of Valletta itself.

Nicholas Upton, who fell defending Malta from the Turks in 1551. Another commemorates those who died in the World War II bombing, when the church's dome was completely destroyed.

Below the church is a new Freedom Monument, unveiled on 31 March 1979, when the British Navy finally departed: it shows a British sailor shaking hands with a Maltese dockworker. The buildings along the waterfront were first used as bakeries by the knights, then by the Royal Navy. Now they house the Maritime Museum.

The site of **Fort St Angelo** had already been built on in Phoenician times with, it is thought, a temple to Astarte, followed by a Greek temple to Hera and a Roman one to Juno. During the Great Siege, the knights moored their galleys in the moat (now largely filled in) between the fort and the town, when St Angelo was their command post. It was also the Royal Navy's headquarters during World War II, and held up well, considering how often it was bombed.

*Carved eyes and ears mark out a lookout post on the walls at Senglea.*

Senglea and Cospicua were also heavily blitzed, and have been rebuilt in modern style as residential areas. **Senglea**, also called l'Isla, was named after the Grand Master who fortified it before the Great Siege, Claude de la Sengle.

Make your way to the little garden at Isola Point, where a look-out tower is aptly sculpted with an eye and an ear.

**Cospicua** (also known as Bormla), is ringed by the formidable multiple walls of the **Cotonera lines**, named after the 17th-century Grand Master Cotoner.

### SLIEMA AND ST JULIAN'S BAY

These are the liveliest spots in Malta for hotels, nightlife and shopping (see pp.66 and 97).

**Sliema**, a thriving suburb of 25,000 people, is a lot larger than Valletta. It's about a 5-km (3-mile) journey from Floriana to Sliema's Strand, passing by or through Pieta, Msida and Ta 'Xbiex, where yachts line the quayside.

Sliema has grown fast in recent years and its general appearance is undistinguished, yet it has good shops, restaurants and a range of hotels. The harbour shore is a concrete promenade, but the rocky north-east coast, facing the open sea, has suitable flat spots for swimming. The peninsula facing Valletta was once a big military base, now being converted to housing and leisure facilities. From the very tip, Dragut Point, the eponymous pirate bombarded St Elmo in the Great Siege.

After St Julian's Point, with its fortified tower, now a café, you reach Balluta Bay, and then **St Julian's Bay**, an old fishing village that has sprouted bars and restaurants. Between here and St George's Bay are luxury hotels, discos, and the Casino. The entire area swarms with bathers on summer weekends.

## Inland to Mdina and Rabat

Mdina is about 12km (7 miles) from Valletta, through busy Hamrun, an industrial suburb. The road passes the **aqueduct**, built in the 17th century by Grand Master Wignacourt and designed to bring water to Valletta. Off to the right from Attard, the **San Anton Gardens** make a refreshing, shady retreat with subtropical trees and flowers, some giant evergreens – possibly descendants of the islands' lusher past when plenty of rain and greenery supported abundant wildlife. At the opposite end of the gardens is the official residence of the President; it was built as a summer palace in the 17th century by Grand Master Antoine de Paule.

Further along the road, also branching off to the right, is Ta' Qali, a former airfield now converted into a crafts village (see p.94).

## MDINA

This historic citadel is one of Malta's most beautiful spots. It may have been inhabited since the Bronze Age, and there were certainly Punic and Roman settlements here.

The Romans called it *Melita* (honey); St Publius, the Roman governor, converted by St Paul and later to become first Bishop of Malta, lived here. When the Arabs fortified the promontory in the 9th century they renamed it *Mdina* (the walled city) and separated it from its 'suburb', Rabat (another word for city).

Also known as *Città Notabile*, Mdina was the first capital of Malta and later the Bishop's See and seat of the Università, the government advisory body. Roger the Norman was greeted here as the island's liberator from the Arabs in 1090. When the knights decided that Valletta should become the capital, Mdina became *Città Vecchia* (meaning 'old city').

Now it is often called 'the silent city', intriguing and secretive with narrow, practically deserted streets. Several of Malta's aristocratic old families still live here – very discreetly in enclosed palaces.

Two main gates (both dated 1724) lead into Mdina. On the left is Greeks' Gate. Take the bridge across the moat from Howard Gardens and enter the town through **Mdina Gate** (the outline of an earlier gate is to the right of it). Just inside, Vilhena Palace is named after the Grand Master who had it built in the 18th century. It currently houses the quaint Museum of

Natural History, whose most interesting exhibit shows the geological 'sandwich' of Malta and Gozo's rock formations.

**Villegaignon Street** is the main thoroughfare throughout, running through to the wall on the other side of town.

To the right is the Convent of St Benedict, a blank-walled building to which men are not admitted. The two churches are St Peter's and St Agatha's. On the left you'll see **Casa Inguanez**, the palace home of Malta's oldest titled family. Typically, the main entrance is in a side street.

The striking **cathedral** (the seat of the bishopric and 'co-cathedral' with St John's in Valletta) is an outstanding baroque work on an island rich in baroque art. Fronted by a pair of cannon, flanked by its two bell towers, it has three doorways with two different types of pilasters (Corinthian below and composite above), making an admirable façade when it is seen from the square. It was built by Lorenzo Gafà between 1697 and 1702 and is considered to be his masterwork.

The interior, under an impressive dome, is well proportioned, yet very rich, and the marble mosaic floor covers the tombs of bishops and notables.

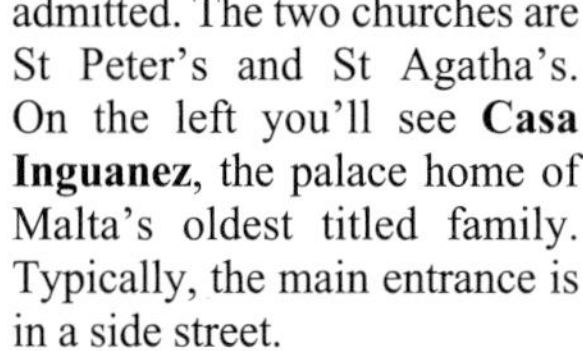

*The Mdina Gate leads to the quiet city where the streets stay mysteriously shady and cool.*

Notice the heavy wooden **doors** through the vestry are carved with snakes and other motifs. A lively **fresco**, *The Shipwreck of St Paul*, by Mattia Preti, is in the apse, and to the left of the apse you'll find a silver **processional cross**, brought to Malta (according to tradition) by the knights from Rhodes.

To the right of the Archbishop's Palace, outside the Cathedral, the former seminary is the **Cathedral Museum**. Its fine **coin collection** will thrill any numismatist. Displayed in mirrored cases, it takes you from Carthage all the way to modern Europe, with stops at many historic moments.

Upstairs is a collection of paintings (Sicilian, Flemish, Spanish, 16th-18th centuries), superb Dürer woodcuts, and delightful engravings by Rembrandt, Piranesi, Van Dyck and Goya. Some beautiful illuminated choirbooks date from as early as the 11th century.

Just off the square in Villegaignon Street, the **Palazzo Santa Sophia**'s ground floor is reputedly the oldest house in

*The dome of Mdina's St Paul's Cathedral, built three centuries ago by Maltese architect Lorenzo Gafà, will impress everyone.*

Mdina, with a typical Maltese feature – a 'string-course' of triangular corbels with balls attached to them. The upper floor was finished 600 years later – to the original plan!

The next big building on the left is the **Church of the Annunciation**. Its bells played an important part in the 1798 revolt against the French, who wanted to sell valuable tapestries belonging to the church, but after an incident during which a young boy attacked the French Commandant Masson, the bells were rung to call people from the neighbouring countryside. After a good deal of brawling, the enraged Maltese threw Masson to his death from the balcony of the notary's house, in one of the first actions of the rebellion that lasted until the French were ousted in 1800.

Near to the end of Villegaignon Street on the right is the **Norman House**, or the Palazzo Falzon. The lower, and earliest part of the house is a defensive façade with only slits for windows (14th-15th centuries). The later and upper section has attractive double-arched windows.

At the end of the street you will come to a large **bastion** with a magnificent **view**, extending to Mosta with its great dome and all the way to the spires of Valletta in the east. Head for Greeks' Gate, diverting along any of the narrow alleys on the way, and you'll see how the city was designed to create cool shade, as well as for defence purposes. Even if enemies penetrated the walls, they could be pelted with missiles from the rooftops, or cut off in dead-end streets.

At **Greeks' Gate**, you can see blocks of Roman masonry in the lower wall, and the outline of an Arab archway, illustrating the long history of this little jewel of a city.

## RABAT

Near the gates of Mdina, the **Roman villa and museum** is worth visiting. This small, columned building made of pinkish stone, and garlanded with rhododendrons, has been built over the mosaic floors and outline walls of the Roman original. Inside, you can see pottery from Carthaginian and Greek tombs as well as some superb Roman glass.

Downstairs in the atrium you'll find the fine mosaics, some made of especially tiny tesserae, which allow for their particular delicately detailed pictures. The adjoining Arab cemetery fortunately managed to just miss the mosaics when its graves were dug.

Rabat itself is Mdina's twin city. **St Augustine's Church**,

*Early Christians cut St Paul's Catacombs, a maze of passages and chambers beneath Rabat.*

found on St Augustine Street, was built by Cassar two years before the cathedral in Valletta. The latter is foreshadowed by the former, especially by its massive barrel-vaulted interior.

In the heart of Rabat, on Parish Square, is the 16th-century **St Paul's Church**, which some think was at least partly the work of Lorenzo Gafà, in particular the big dome.

Next to the church (on the left, downstairs) is the entrance to **St Paul's Grotto**, where the saint supposedly took shelter when he was in Malta. Legend has it that no matter how much stone was extracted from the cave, by some miracle it always grew back.

The **catacombs** (St Paul's and St Agatha's; signs point the way) are cool mazes of galleries and passageways. Their extent suggests that a large Christian community lived in the area in the 4th and 5th centuries. The circular stone platforms are thought to have been tables for funeral feasts where guests reclined in the Roman style, and some of the chambers seem to have been used for prayer meetings. St Agatha's catacombs show traces of frescoes depicting saints, doves and shell designs.

*A heraldic painted ceiling in Verdala Castle, formerly the Grand Masters' summer palace.*

## VERDALA, BUSKETT, DINGLI

Take the road from Rabat to Buskett, and **Verdala Castle** lies just east off the road, a few minutes from Rabat. It is open on Tuesdays and Fridays, with tours conducted by the curator, and is well worth a visit. Once the summer residence of Grand

Cart tracks (left) were made by dragging sleds full of stones. Sightseers travel by today's form of transport to the 'Blue Grotto'.

Masters and Governors, it is now an occasional retreat for the President and guests. Gerolamo Cassar built this square castle surrounded by a moat and pine groves in 1586 for the Grand Master de Verdalle, Cardinal Verdala. It has a magnificent elliptical **staircase** and a superb view from the roof.

The **Buskett** or *Boschetto* (meaning 'little wood') is one of the island's greenest spots, where the knights raised their falcons for hunting. On 28 and 29 June, Malta's folklore festival is held here. These woods are also the setting for Girgenti, the summer palace of the Inquisitor, a good place to relax from his weighty duties. (It is not open to visitors.)

At nearby **Dingli Cliffs**, a sheer drop of 250m (800ft) down to the sea gives a dizzying view. The islet in the distance is Filfla, made even smaller by the British who used it for bombing practice.

Between the Buskett Gardens and the cliffs, signs to 'Clapham Junction' (a joke reference to the busiest London train station) direct you to one of the best areas to see prehistoric '**cart ruts**' (see p.12). A broad rocky slope is grooved in rectangles where great stones were quarried, and deep, curving double tracks lead down the hill. They were made by some kind of sled on which the stones were dragged away.

# South-East Coast

**Ghar Lapsi** is a mere cluster of buildings under the cliffs, but it is one of the few ways down to the sea near here, so the tiny beach is a local favourite. Further east, by the road to Żurrieq, is Malta's **Blue Grotto** – not as large as Capri's, nor as crowded. The approach road offers some spectacular views and leads to a small car park, where you'll find boatmen in their colourful water taxis ready to shuttle you round the point and into the limestone caves. Try to go in the morning before 10 o'clock, when sunlight slants into the caves to reflect off the white sandy bottom. In some places your hand will glow turquoise blue if you drag it in the water.

The 25-minute excursion takes in several caves, where the limestone is tinted pink, mauve and orange by coral

and minerals, especially in one called 'Reflection Cave'. In the best light, the Blue Grotto itself is a luminous, pure blue, and a square natural 'window' in the rock gives the effect of a fluorescent lamp.

While you're in the area, you could visit the twin temple sites of Hagar Qim and Mnajdra, which are close at hand on the cliff top (see pp.73 and 74).

**Marsaxlokk**, on an eastern arm of Marsaxlokk Bay, is the largest fishing village in Malta, colourful and peaceful, with bobbing *luzzu* boats, fishermen mending their nets, and a good choice of seafood restaurants around the harbour. Within the

*The bay of Marsaxlokk, with its calm blue waters, was probably what first attracted Napoleon here in 1798.*

larger bay, St George's Bay is the site of Ghar Dalam (see p.64) and Pretty Bay was once a favourite local holiday haunt – industry and modern installations have made it less worthy of its name.

Dragut the pirate landed in Marsaxlokk in 1565, and in the 17th century several defensive towers were built. This didn't deter Napoleon, whose troops disembarked here in 1798. In more modern times the bay was a seaplane base.

A small road running down to **Delimara Point** takes you past Tas-Silġ Chapel, where there is a Carmelite Monastery, and the site of a Punic-Roman temple. You can swim from the rocks at Peter's Pool but St Thomas Bay is shallow, sandy and popular with windsurfers. Between the two, at Xrobb Il-Għagin are some vestiges of a Neolithic temple.

**Marsaskala**, at the head of its own narrow bay, is like a smaller Marsaxlokk, complete with pastel houses and colourful fishing boats. Rapid building in recent years has lined the inlet with apartments and villas and, where it meets the sea, one of Malta's biggest hotels.

# The North West

Although relatively fertile, this part of Malta was once difficult to defend, and so was underpopulated. Its sandy beaches are now a big attraction.

As you're heading this way, you will hardly miss one of the island's outstanding landmarks, the **dome** of the parish church in the busy little town of **Mosta**. St Mary's was built with local money and by voluntary labour between 1833-60 to the designs of the architect Giorgio de Vassé, and the inhabitants are justly proud of it.

The magnificent, enormous dome, whose 37m (123ft) diameter makes it one of the largest in the world, was constructed without the use of scaffolding. Behind a classical façade, the impression inside is one of 'all dome', surrounded by apses. The geometrical marble floor heightens the effect. A bomb fell through the dome on 9 April 1942, sliding across the floor without exploding – a miracle for those present. A replica of the bomb stands in the sacristy on the left.

North west from Sliema and St Julian's, **St Andrew's** was once a huge army base, now converted into civilian housing and holiday facilities. The road runs alongside the coast again at Bahar ic-Cagħaq, where there is a waterslide park. After several headlands and old towers, you arrive at **Salina Bay**, with a small playground, salt pans and reedbeds. Further round the bay at **Qawra** (remember – the Q is almost silent), big resort hotels and beach clubs offer plenty of watersports facilities.

Next, by rounding Qawra Point, where the knights' fort is now a restaurant, or by cutting across the peninsula, you will come to **St Paul's Bay**. On its south side, **Buġibba** village and the town of San Pawl il-Bahar have grown together into a major holiday resort, with watersports and swimming from the rocks or small sandy beaches. Hotels, apartments, restaurants, bars and discos have sprung up, but traditional life continues too, in the old parts of town and the fishing harbour.

St Paul came ashore near here after he was shipwrecked in AD 60. The legend goes that it was on the larger of the two islands you can see over the water. Għajn Razul ('apostle's fountain') is said to be where he struck a rock, which miraculously brought forth water.

Mistra Bay is an inlet within St Paul's Bay, on the opposite shore from the town and

*The immense dome of Mosta's church is justly proud of its title as one of the world's biggest.*

harbour. Reached by a road through the rural landscape and reedbeds of Kalkara Ravine, it has the attraction of a sandy, although sometimes weed-covered beach.

For some really fine views, walk the rocky tracks round the headland facing St Paul's Islands, and hike or drive up to Selmun Palace, the knights' redoubt on the hilltop.

**Mellieħa Bay**, just under Marfa Ridge (the 'tail' of fish-shaped Malta), is the biggest stretch of sandy beach in the islands, and likely to be crowded in the high season. Perched on the commanding spur of Mellieħa Ridge, the town of **Mellieħa** itself has a superb view of Marfa Ridge and Comino with Gozo stretching beyond. The stone church stands like a reddish fortress on the promontory. It dates from the 18th century, but nestling within is a chapel from the early Middle Ages, now a site of pilgrimage. A small chapel next to the church contains a painting of the Virgin said to be by St Luke.

To drive or walk along **Marfa Ridge** is almost like flying, the views in all directions are so spectacular. The knights' Red Tower (1649) is the most prominent of the defence posts from various eras that dot the ridge. On its northern shore, you'll find stretches of sandy beach and hotels at Armier, Ramla and Paradise

*Local tradition says St Paul first came ashore on the island across the bay which bears his name.*

Bays. Ċirkewwa is the landing stage where you can take the car ferry for the 20-minute crossing to Gozo.

Across the narrow neck of land from Mellieħa Bay, rocky but beautiful **Anchor Bay** was so named because it once had large anchors on the shore. Children will be thrilled to discover the engagingly ramshackle **Popeye Village**, constructed there as the set for the film *Popeye* and retained as a tourist attraction. A small admission fee is charged, but you can then use the beach for as long as you like.

**Golden Bay** (*Ramla Tal-Mixquqa*) is a broad crescent of sand, not always pristine clean, with a good selection of cafés and a big tourist complex on the hillside just above.

The much smaller Għajn Tuffieha Bay just next door, reached via a long staircase, attracts (and can take) fewer swimmers than Golden Bay. Inland to the south, you'll find the interesting remains of a Roman bath-house. Charming **Ġnejna Bay**, with its colourful boathouses cut into the cliffs, has a sheltered, calm sandy beach.

# The Prehistoric Sites

Malta's prehistory is impressive and enigmatic. The settlement by humans began with the arrival of agricultural immigrants who came from Sicily around the year 5000 BC. Futher waves of immigrants followed and the corresponding phases of development have been classified and given names which you'll encounter both at prehistoric sites and in museums.

All prehistoric dates must be regarded as approximate. Those quoted here agree with the latest available research, including the technique of dendrochronology (or tree-ring dating), which gives dates substantially earlier than the results from carbon-14 testing that were accepted hitherto.

The different stages of Maltese prehistoric civilization have been called after the important sites associated with them, such as: the **Għar Dalam** period, lasting up to about 4500 BC; the **Skorba** period, 4500- 4100 BC; the **Żebbuġ** period (3900 BC); the **Mġarr** period (3700 BC) and the **Ġgantija** period (3600-3000 BC). Outstanding in this latter are the temples at Ġgantija on Gozo (see p.81), Ħaġar Qim, and an early temple at Tarxien. The **Hal Saflieni Hypogeum** is a remarkable complex possibly dating back to 3300 BC and continuing in use through the **Tarxien** period (around 3200-2500 BC), which left impressive temples at Tarxien itself, Mnajdra, Skorba and Borġ in-Nadur.

Then, around 2500 BC, an unexplained sudden end came to temple-building. Drought and starvation, emigration, religious hysteria and mass suicide have all been guessed at as reasons for this mystery.

The next group of immigrants used Tarxien as a cemetery from 2500-1500 BC – they're called the **Cemetery People**. Around 1500 BC, the **Borġ in-Nadur** (Bronze Age) period began with the last group of migrants to arrive – until the Phoenicians came in about 800 BC.

*At Ħaġar Qim on the south coast, the megalithic temples go back over 5,000 years.*

Few hard facts are known about the religion practised by the temple-builders. Phallic symbols and their female equivalent, triangles, the huge, fat and skirted figure at Tarxien (the original is in the Valletta National Museum) and various smaller versions would seem to suggest a fertility cult.

The temples' curved outer walls were usually made of hard coralline limestone with faces or edges of blocks alternately projecting. Then came a packing of rubble and the inner walls, usually of globigerina limestone. Doorways and passages were erected on the trilithon principle – resembling posts and lintel.

Most temples were built in lobes or apses around a central court or passage. Common features included altars, possible 'oracle chambers' and hollowed stones, perhaps used for collecting libations of blood from sacrificial animals. There was usually also a massive, concave front wall with an impressive entrance. Early temple interiors and altars had a pitted decoration and later there were carvings, which must have been done with stone, since no corresponding metal tools have been found.

During the Bronze Age, sophisticated metal-working techniques came to the islands, but the new immigrants produced nothing comparable to the earlier achievements, many of which pre-date other ancient wonders such as the Great Pyramid and Stonehenge. Maltese construction techniques are considered unique: it seems the builders invented everything themselves.

The following are some of the more interesting temples and caves to be visited. Go early in the morning if you want to avoid crowds (and be cool) and go with a qualified guide if you don't want to miss a lot of subtle details.

About 10km (6 miles) from Valletta, **Għar Dalam** is an important cave site. The small museum there shows the types of animals that existed on Malta in the Pleistocene era.

**Prehistoric Economics**

How were the tombs and temples of ancient Malta built and financed? The evidence suggests that the islanders lived peaceably together without much trouble from outsiders, and agriculture provided for the needs of the quite small population.

A tribal system with tithes paid to the chief would have made possible a structured society, able to pay priests and artisans, as well as providing organized labour to construct temples.

The people imported flint and obsidian to be used as tools, for these were not locally available. How they paid for imports is still unknown, though the medium of exchange may have been something perishable, perhaps textiles or possibly even elaborate temple robes.

# A Selection of Hotels and Restaurants in Malta

# Recommended Hotels

Hotel prices have risen in recent years, but they are still quite reasonable by the standards of many Mediterranean destinations. Most hotels are concentrated in a few areas, alongside holiday apartments, some time-shares and a few villas. Since distances are short, everywhere on Malta is easily accessible – and even more so on Gozo.

Some of the hotels that cater for groups may be full from May to October, and the season seems to be getting longer. A few close for the mid-winter months. If buying a package holiday, remember that some hotels play safe and serve a rather dull and bland diet. If you go for half-board, you'll be free to try the wide variety of other eating places.

Our Berlitz choice, listed alphabetically, area by area, is made with the help of experienced travellers and island residents, taking account of quality, location, price and character. It is not meant to be exclusive: we don't have space for all the good places, and new ones are opening up all the time.

As a basic guide, we have used the symbols below to indicate the price for a double room with bath or shower, including breakfast. Winter prices are often significantly less. (Note that Maltese hotels usually quote a rate *per person*.)

| | |
|---|---|
| **III** | above Lm 25 |
| **II** | Lm 15-25 |
| **I** | below Lm 15 |

## VALLETTA AREA AND THE SOUTH EAST

**Alfonso** **II**

*Triq il Qaġhliet, St Julian's Bay*
*Tel. 310437*

Charming hotel very near to the fun in St Julian's – nightclubs, restaurants, discos and the International Casino de Malte. Sun terrace with panoramic views.

**Castille** **II**

*Castile Square, Valletta*
*Tel. 243677/9*
*Fax 243679*

Close to City Gate and Upper Barrakka Gardens, in a restored 16th/17th-century house. Rooftop terrace.

**Fortina** **III**

*Tigne Sea Front, Sliema*
*Tel. 343380*
*Fax 332004*
Modern block with fine views facing south near Dragut Point. Swimming pools, watersports, gym with fitness facilities, tennis. Entertainment.

**Health Farm** **II**

*62 Main Street, Tarxien*
*Tel. 666477*
Old-established retreat in converted and extended stone hunting lodge. Pools, gardens, squash, tennis and a wide variety of treatments and therapies.

**Hilton International** **III**

*Spinola, St Julian's*
*Tel. 336201*
*Fax 341539*
Modern resort hotel with a host of facilities. Gardens, pools, watersports. Swimming from rocky shore. Tennis. Disco-bar.

**Holiday Inn Crowne Plaza** **III**

*Tigne Sea Front, Sliema*
*Tel. 341173/9*
*Fax 311292*
Stunning views of Marsamxett Harbour from this luxury hotel. Three restaurants, gym, sauna, tennis courts, squash, indoor and outdoor pools, piano bar. 182 rooms all with good facilities.

**Imperial** **II**

*Rudolphe Street, Sliema*
*Tel. 344762*
*Fax 336471*
Comfortable hotel in an older part of Sliema, a short walk from the waterfront. Sundeck and pool.

**Jerma Palace** **III**

*Marsaskala*
*Tel. 823222*
*Fax 829485*
Large and spectacular resort hotel on a rocky point near the fishing harbour of Marsaskala. Bars, restaurant and nightclub. Swimming pools, watersports and variety of fitness facilities.

**Kennedy Court** **II**

*166 The Strand, Sliema*
*Tel. 314668*
*Fax 493900*
South/harbour-facing bright and modern hotel. Pool, roof terrace, health and fitness facilities.

**Marina** **I**

*Tigne Sea Front, Sliema*
*Tel. 336461*
*Fax 330650*

Tall, functional block facing harbour. Rooftop terrace.

**Milano Due** **II**
*The Strand, Gzira, nr Sliema*
*Tel. 345040/4*
*Fax 345045*
Bright, modern harbourside block. Simple rooms. Delightful rooftop restaurant.

## ST PAUL'S BAY AND THE NORTH

**Concorde** **I**
*Pioneer Road, Buġibba*
*Tel. 573831*
*Fax 473292*
New block near seafront, with modern, simply equipped rooms. Pool, private beach.

**Golden Sands** **II**
*Golden Bay, Għajn Tuffeiha*
*Tel. 573961*
*Fax 580875*
Big resort hotel on the cliff above the beautiful sandy bay. Pools, watersports, diving, tennis, entertainment.

**Liliana** **II**
*Tirq ic-Centurjun, Buġibba*
*Tel. 572319*
*Fax 473292*
80 rooms in pleasant hotel. Close to Roosendaal lido complex with pool which guests staying at the Liliana can use freely.

**New Dolmen** **III**
*Promenade, Buġibba*
*Tel. 581510*
*Fax 581532*
Very large resort hotel and sports complex on St Paul's Bay. Pools, tennis, squash, watersports, fitness facilities, entertainment. Neolithic site within gardens. Conference centre.

**Qawra Palace** **II**
*Qawra Coast, Qawra*
*Tel. 580131/2*
*Fax 472610*
Big, modern resort hotel opposite rocky shore. Pools, watersports, fitness facilities.

**Ramla Bay** **III**
*Ramla Bay, Marfa*
*Tel. 573521/3*
*Fax 575931*
At the northern tip of Malta, by its own small, private, sandy beach and rocky shore. Good facilities with pools, watersports, tennis and entertainment.

**Suncrest** **III**
*Salina Bay, Qawra*
*Tel. 477101*
*Fax 475478*
424 twin rooms each with balcony and most with good sea views.

Outdoor pools, five restaurants, nightclub, cocktails, watersports centre, and floodlit tennis.

## RABAT/MDINA AND THE SOUTH WEST

### Grand Hotel Verdala III

*Inguanez Street, Rabat*
*Tel. 451700/7*
*Fax 461708*
Hilltop retreat convenient for Mdina, with comfortable, traditional rooms. Gardens, pools, and a disco.

### Palazzo Costanzo I

*Villegaignon Street, Mdina*
*Tel. 456301*
*Fax 454625*
Small guest house in an old building on a quiet street.

## GOZO AND COMINO

### Atlantis I

*Marsalforn, Gozo*
*Tel. 554685*
*Fax 555661*
Small, modern block a couple of minutes' walk from the bay.

### Calypso II

*Marsalforn, Gozo*
*Tel. 562000/9*
*Fax 562012*
Big, modern, functional block by the harbour. Pool, watersports, diving, tennis, squash. Disco and Chinese restaurant.

### Comino III

*Island of Comino*
*Tel. 529822/5*
*Fax 529826*
Self-contained resort with many facilities. Pools, watersports, diving, tennis courts, disco. Closed November-March.

### Cornucopia II

*Gnien Imrik, Xagħra, Gozo*
*Tel. 556486*
*Fax 552910*
Converted farmhouse with attractive, modern rooms in extensions around gardens and pools, just outside little hilltop town.

### Serena I

*St Simon Street, Xlendi, Gozo*
*Tel. 557452*
Apartment hotel (breakfast available) with pleasant, bright rooms on cliff above the inlet. Rooftop pool and terrace. Watersports.

### Ta' Ċenċ III

*Sennat, Gozo*
*Tel. 551520/1*
*Fax 588199*
Luxury accommodation with 85 rooms. Two outdoor pools, indoor heated pool and health facilities.

# Recommended Restaurants

To give a rough guide to the price of a three-course meal with wine, restaurants are classified as follows:

| | |
|---|---|
| III | above Lm10 |
| II | Lm 5-10 |
| I | below 5 Lm |

You can, of course, eat a filling plate of pasta or a local dish for very much less, and some medium-priced restaurants offer a 'tourist menu' for Lm 2-3. Service is normally included in restaurant prices, although 10% government tax is added. A tip of 10-15% is expected for good service.

Unless otherwise stated, the restaurants listed below are open daily for lunch and dinner. We do not attempt to list beach cafés, fast-food outlets and bars serving food, good value though they may be. They number in their hundreds.

## VALLETTA AREA AND THE SOUTH EAST

**Bologna** **II**
*59 Republic Street, Valletta*
*Tel. 246149*
City-centre setting. Italian cuisine. Closed Sundays and public holidays.

**Bouzouki** **II**
*Gort Street, Paceville, St Julian's*
*Tel. 317127*
Greek cuisine. Informal setting. Closed lunchtime and Sundays.

**Café Cordina** **I**
*244 Republic Street, Valletta*
*Tel. 234385*
Light meals and snacks in a bright city-centre setting.

**Carriage** **III**
*The Strand, Sliema*
*Tel. 333864/334398*
In elegant town house, or garden setting in summer. Excellent international cuisine. Closed lunchtimes, Sundays and public holidays.

**Cotton Club** **II**
*Dragonara Road, Paceville, St Julian's*
*Tel. 319347*
Pasta and other Italian dishes. Upstairs in modern block, next to its own disco.

**Fisherman's Rest** **II**
*St Thomas Bay, Żejtun*
*Tel. 822049/681763*
Fish and international cuisine, in an informal, waterside setting. Closed Mondays.

**Il'Ghonella** **II**
*Spinola Palace, St Julian's*
*Tel. 341027*
Set in cellars of old palace. International and Italian menu. Closed Tuesdays.

**Il-Parapett** **I**
*St George's Road, St Julian's*
*Tel. 333394*
Italian and Maltese dishes and snacks. Cheerful and informal atmosphere.

**La Veneziana** **I**
*29-30 Melita Street, Valletta*
*Tel. 222513*
Snacks and pizzas. Informal café, convenient for city centre.

**Mangal** **II**
*Tigne Sea Front, Sliema*
*Tel. 342174/347046*
In Fortina Hotel on waterfront. Authentic Turkish cuisine and grills. Closed lunchtime July and August.

**San Giuliano** **III**
*3 St Joseph Street, St Julian's*
*Tel. 332000*
Elegantly situated right over the harbour. Wide range of Italian dishes. Closed Monday lunchtime.

**Skuna II** **II**
*4 Duncan Street, Marsaxlokk*
*Tel. 871575*
Informal restaurant near harbour. Fish specialities. Closed Tuesday and public holidays.

**Winston** **II**
*16 High Street, Sliema*
*Tel. 334584*
Fish and international menu in an elegant setting – garden in summer. Closed Sundays.

## ST PAUL'S BAY AND THE NORTH

**Arches** **III**
*113 Main Street, Mellieħa*
*Tel. 573436/520533*
Widely known for inventive French and international cuisine. Closed lunchtime and Sundays.

**Cross Keys** **I**
*Cross Square, Mellieħa*
*Tel. 572587*
Lively, with varied international dishes and snacks. Evenings only.

**Gillieru** **II**
*Church Street, St Paul's Bay*
*Tel. 573480/573269*

Large harbourside restaurant. Fish and international dishes.

**It-Tokk** **II**
*Qawra Coast, Qawra*
*Tel. 577101*
In Suncrest Hotel. Specializing in Maltese dishes, including *antipasti* on a real *luzzu* fishing boat.

**Portobello** **II**
*St Luke Street, Buġibba*
*Tel. 571661*
Pasta, fish and international cooking. On terrace over the water.

**Savini** **II**
*Qawra Road, Salina Bay*
*Tel. 576927*
Wide range of Italian cuisine in old house with roof terrace. Closed Sundays.

**Ta' Cassia** **II**
*Qawra Road, Salina Bay*
*Tel. 571435*
In old farmhouse. Maltese, pasta and fish dishes. Evenings only.

## RABAT/MDINA AND THE SOUTH WEST

**Bacchus** **II**
*Inguanez Alley, Mdina*
*Tel. 454981/459437*
International, Italian and Maltese dishes in attractive old mansion.

**Gusman's Birdcage** **II**
*22 Gusman Navarra Street, Rabat*
*Tel. 454052*
Fish dishes and Maltese cuisine. Informal cellar setting. Closed Sundays.

**Medina** **III**
*7 Holy Cross Street, Mdina*
*Tel. 454004*
Set in fine old house, using courtyard in summer. French, international and Maltese menu.Closed Sundays and public holidays.

## GOZO AND COMINO

**Auberge Chez Amand** **II**
*Victoria to Għarb road, Gozo*
*Tel. 551197/555179*
French and international cuisine, in extended old house.

**Auberge Ta' Frenc** **III**
*Marsalforn Road, between Victoria and Marsalforn, Gozo*
*Tel. 554668/553888*
Old farmhouse, attractively extended. French and international cuisine. Closed Monday, Friday and Sunday lunchtime.

**Forchetta** **II**
*Qolla Street, Marsalforn, Gozo*
*Tel. 556203*
Cheerful, informal restaurant. Italian cuisine and snacks.

The exhibits include hippopotami and dwarf elephants. At one time the sea covered Malta, then it receded greatly, probably leaving at first a land bridge to Sicily, by which the large animals crossed. As the climate grew drier and food became scarcer, the number of animals gradually dwindled, and dwarf varieties developed. Animal bones and later human remains were found in the cave, a short walk downhill.

Uncovered from the late 19th century on, the natural cave intercepts a *wied*, or ravine, carved out of the hill by rushing water. Layers of detritus, including bones of wild animals, were washed down the ravine and into the cave. Human bones and carbonized grains found in upper layers show that the cave was inhabited in Neolithic times and that these earliest settlers were agricultural people. The cave is cool and restful, but there's not much to see except a few stalactites and stalagmites.

Less than a mile away, on the way to St George's Bay, is **Borġ in-Nadur**, a village that was fortified around 1500 BC, with some remaining ruins of houses and 'cart-ruts' (see p. 12) nearby. The strong defensive wall includes stones from earlier temples.

**Skorba** at Żebbiegħ is the oldest dwelling site in Malta, with a wall built before 4000 BC, and the remains of farmers' and herdsmen's huts and two megalithic temples.

Ħaġar Qim and Mnajdra, about 13km (8 miles) from Valletta, can be reached via Żurrieq or Siggiewi. The site of **Ħaġar Qim** is spectacular – high above the sea, with a view of Filfla island. You'll see the typical concave façade of the main temple and a complex series of rooms. Unusually, this temple is almost entirely built of the softer globigerina limestone, so it is eroded and weathered.

Interesting details include tethering loops for animals in the stone near the entrance, various 'mushroom' or 'tea-table' altars in the second court, and other altars with the early pitted decoration. The lower half of one of the famous 'fat lady' figures was found in this temple, a skirted cult figure with piano legs now in the National Museum (see p.62).

**Mnajdra** is a five-minute walk down a stone causeway towards the sea, in an even more beautiful setting. The temples here are contemporary with Ħaġar Qim and the two sites have many features in common, but at Mnajdra, the stone is particularly subtly worked and curved. Look for the remarkable multiple doorways and the cleverly cut oracle holes and, for an overview,

*Multiple stone doorways of a temple at Mnajdra, near Ħaġar Qim, from where there are good views of Filfla island.*

climb a short way up the hill behind the site.

The **Hal Saflieni Hypogeum** (a Greek word meaning 'underground') is in **Paola**, a southern suburb of Valletta. This eerie labyrinth, carved from soft limestone, is vast and overwhelming, not recommended for sufferers of claustrophobia. It was hollowed out on three different levels, the deepest plunging to a depth of 12m (40ft), and was discovered by accident when workers were digging cisterns for new houses in 1902. Professionally explored by archaeologist Sir Themistocles Zammit, it is one of Europe's most fascinating prehistoric sites.

You descend by a modern spiral staircase into near-darkness. The first level would seem to be the oldest and cut the roughest (around 3300 BC). The two lower levels were made around the time of the Tarxien Temples (3200-2500 BC) and were carved out with increasing care and sophistication. The middle level has imitation corbelling, and doors and niches cleverly copying the features of the above-ground temples. The Oracle Chamber has a hollow where men (and only men, it seems) can make an odd echo effect. In the Main Chamber, the 'sleeping lady' statuette (now in the National Museum) was found. Some rooms have red or black decoration in spirals or hexagons; one wall drawing is meant to be a bull.

The whole complex covers an area of 800sq m (8,600sq ft) and is estimated to have contained 7,000 bodies. Sheltered from attack by the outside elements, this is undoubtedly ancient Malta's best-preserved monument.

Only 400m (1,300ft) away, the **Tarxien** temples date from the same era as the lower levels of the Hal Saflieni Hypogeum, but their garden setting makes a complete contrast. The temples were discovered by a farmer who was having trouble ploughing his fields with all the megalithic stones in his way: on hearing of this, the archaeologist Sir Themistocles Zammit jumped at the chance to uncover the site, which was excavated between 1915 and 1919.

The temples were built at different times, from about 3200-2500 BC. On the way in you'll see a plan of the area, some replicas of carved stones and another piano-legged 'fat lady' statue. The first temple you come to has replicas of lively bas-relief carvings – spirals, sheep, goats, pigs, cattle, and the lower half of yet another 'fat lady', whose vast thighs are an inspiration to any weight-watcher.

The second temple is original in having six lobes or oval bays off the main axis, instead of the more usual four or five. Part of the floor has been removed to show some of the hundreds of heavy stone balls used as rollers for the huge slabs – they were left in place as supports.

The third temple of the group is the oldest with, a little further on, parts of the ancient Ġgantija-period temple.

## Gozo

The legendary siren Calypso kept Ulysses enthralled here for seven blissful years, and Gozo still enchants people who like its sleepy pace and rustic charm. In the local language, it's known as *Għawdex* (pronounced 'Ow-dehsh').

Malta's smaller sister is only 14km (9 miles) long by 7km (4 miles) wide, boasts a population of almost 30,000, and its own distinctive character. Gozitans are proud of their island and quite tolerant of Maltese jokes depicting them as country cousins. They can afford to be: many have made it to the top in business, government and the Church, in Malta and the world beyond.

Gozo is greener than Malta, with neat terraces, dry stone walls and big flat-topped hills. In every direction, the towers and domes of churches are silhouetted against the sky. The islanders are great church-builders: many of the parish churches are big enough for a city of half a million people, not to mention the dozens of little wayside chapels. A day in Gozo is constantly punctuated by church bells ringing their various messages.

While 20th-century traffic has taken over the few main roads, life still goes on much as it did a century ago. For one thing, big agricultural equipment can't be delivered, and wouldn't be much use on the narrow terraces if it could. Gozo lives mainly on farming, with excellent crops of tomatoes, potatoes, melons, oranges and figs. The fishing fleet puts to sea whenever the weather permits and, despite declining stocks, still manages to bring in a tasty and varied catch.

Activity centres around the hub and capital, Victoria, although there is much to see elsewhere. Gozo has not only interesting baroque and other churches, but also the great Neolithic temples of Ġgantija, and spectacular scenery. Beach life can be beautiful here, but it's also simple: you won't find a sophisticated cabana setting. There are few luxury hotels, but some of the small hotels and restaurants are delightful, and a growing number of farmhouses are being converted into holiday homes.

Gozo does not run to an airstrip, only a helicopter pad. However, you can reach the island either by ferry from Sa Maison, near Valletta, or from Ċirkewwa, on a private boat or on an excursion from Sliema – whichever route you take, the short crossing is a pleasure. You'll pass Comino with its watchtower: the island's one hotel stands above a bay on the other side. The name Comino comes from the herb cumin, which once grew in abundance there. The uninhabited islet of Cominetto partly shields Comino's idyllic Blue Lagoon – a magnet for excursion boats in summer – and minutes later you've arrived.

**Mġarr** is everything an island harbour should be, alive with bobbing *luzzu* boats and visiting yachts. The tall steeple on the hill above belongs to a 19th-century church, Our Lady of Lourdes. On the headland is Fort Chambray, built in the mid-18th century by a French knight.

The ups and downs of Gozo's history broadly reflect Malta's. First the builders of prehistoric temples at Ġgantija, then the Phoenicians, Romans, Arabs and Normans, Turkish raiders, the Knights of St John and finally the British – all have left their mark.

By the side of the road between Mġarr and Victoria, **Gozo Heritage** is a cleverly designed evocation of island history. You are led by sound and lights through a series of rooms, each one a dramatic tableau. (There's an admission charge.) In an adjoining shop you can sometimes has crafts-people working.

## VICTORIA

The British renamed Gozo's bustling centre during Queen Victoria's jubilee in 1897, but Gozitans still use its old Arab name, Rabat ('city').

Just 6km (4 miles) from Mġarr, the town has a citadel standing high on a bluff: it's a landmark visible from most parts of the island.

The broad main street is **Republic Street** (Racecourse Street) with the bank and post office. During the Feast of the Assumption on 15 August, nearby Rundle Gardens are the scene of a charming country fair. During the same period (and also on the Feast of St George, on the third Sunday in July) colourful horse and donkey races are run, when everybody turns out to see their friends race in sulkies or ride bareback up Republic Street: it can be hilarious.

**It-Tokk**, the attractive tree-shaded square, with its war monument in the middle, is edged with little shops, tunnel-shaped bars and a bank. On one side is the 18th-century St James's Church, on the other a rounded building, dating from 1733, which once housed the Banca Giuratala: today it's an information office and a haven for locals wishing to read their newspapers.

During festival times, the square becomes a riot of colour with various religious statues: 'Judas' pointedly stands just outside the Inland Revenue Office and there are garlands everywhere. But any morning it's full of activity from the open-air market. In the evenings it swarms with people again, walking slowly up and down for the *passeggiata,* or social hour.

At market times, you'll see a lavish display of fish, fruit and vegetables, and hear lively banter between shoppers and sellers. The **old town** behind It-Tokk is charmingly picturesque, with narrow alleys, simple old houses, and women making lace in their doorways. In St George's Street almost every house has a plaque of the saint slaying the dragon.

On its eponymous square, **St George's Church** is a fine example of baroque architecture, elaborately gilded and decorated. The **painting** by Mattia Preti over the choir altar shows St George with his foot

*Mġarr, Gozo's charming little harbour, is where ferries and hydrofoils arrive from Malta.*

victoriously poised on the dragon's head, his white charger by his side. The July festival is quite a bash, and there is a good deal of rivalry between St George's Church and the cathedral, whose festival is the Assumption, on 15 August.

The **cathedral** stands within the citadel. Behind the austere stone façade, guarded by two bronze cannons, is a surprisingly elaborate interior. Built by Lorenzo Gafà between 1697 and 1711, it has a convincing *trompe l'oeil* dome painted by Antonio Manuele; the real dome was never finished for lack of funds.

On the left as you enter is a modern statue of the Virgin in pale blue and white, her eyes and hands raised heavenward, posed on an ornate and heavy silver pedestal. It is carried all around town during the Festival of the Assumption. The Cathedral Museum at the back houses collections of church ornaments, sacred vestments and paintings.

To the south of the Cathedral stands the Bondi Palace, containing the **Gozo Museum of Archeology** built around an inner courtyard. Among the exhibits are Punic jewellery, *amphorae* (jars) from Roman shipwrecks, the 12th-century tombstone of an Arab girl, Majnuna, with a touching inscription, and shards and relics from various eras, especially prehistoric phases.

*Steep steps lead up to the Cathedral within the citadel at Victoria on Gozo.*

A model of Ġgantija as well as a large phallic symbol from one of Ġgantija's temples will provide a good introduction to the temples you can see at Xaghra.

Up a little street on the other side of the cathedral, you'll come to the **Folklore Museum** where some traditional implements and costumes are displayed in three restored old houses. Further up this alley, and also by practically every other path, there are steps leading to the ramparts of the **citadel**. In the 15-minute walk around them you will be presented with marvellous **views** all over Gozo, with flat-topped houses edging the meandering roads and a church on nearly every hilltop. The ramparts were strengthened after the brutal Turkish incursion and kidnappings of 1551.

After failing in an assault against the knights in Malta, Dragut, the North African pirate (see p.20), attacked Gozo, carrying off almost the whole population of 6,000 islanders to slavery. Gozo was invaded many times by the Turks in the 16th century and gradually the stone dwellings of the citadel were abandoned. Though the rubble where goats graze looks as deserted as Ġgantija, there are plans for its restoration.

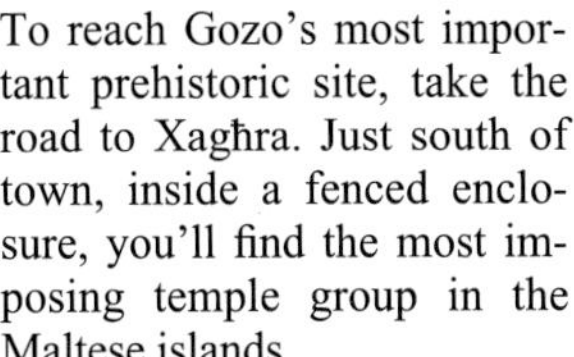

## ĠGANTIJA TEMPLES

To reach Gozo's most important prehistoric site, take the road to Xagħra. Just south of town, inside a fenced enclosure, you'll find the most imposing temple group in the Maltese islands.

Ġgantija was excavated at various times between 1827-1953. Like most prehistoric temples in Malta, the two here face south east: the older and larger is on the left as you approach them. It dates back to 3600-3300 BC (see p.62 for a comment on dating), during the period sometimes called the Copper Age (precursor to the Bronze Age), though there was no copper on Malta or Gozo then.

Typical of this type of temple, the façade is slightly concave. The entry is flanked by two orthostats (upright stones), a big slab, and a concave stone where worshippers may have washed their feet. The left part of the façade is made of immense coralline limestone slabs which rise to a height of about 6m (20ft).

The inside walls and decoration are of the softer globigerina limestone. Five lobe-shaped apses contain a number of interesting features, including libation holes, an oracle hole and stones carved with swirling patterns.

One stone block once supported the huge phallic symbol which now resides in the Gozo National Museum. The three rear apses were probably restricted to priests and the end apse has impressively high walls, which curve inward to make a semi-dome. The altar, with holes perhaps used for draining animal blood, has blocks with pitted decoration, typical of the period.

The smaller and later temple is less interesting. Here the rear apse and altar are a mere niche. A walk round the whole site shows the skill of early builders. Some of the huge blocks of limestone measure 5.5m (18ft) long and weigh up to 50 tonnes. You can only marvel at the technical feat performed by a people supposedly knowing no mathematics, in raising these structures.

## TOWNS AND VILLAGES

**Xagħra**, north west of Ġgantija, was inhabited in prehistoric times. It's a pleasant town with an exuberantly decorated, baroque 19th-century church. Signs point to Xerri's Cave and Ninu's Cave, which you can visit if you would like to see odd-shaped stalactites and stalagmites.

At the north-east corner of the Xagħra plateau, with its superb view over to Ramla Bay on the right, you come to **Calypso's Cave**, where Ulysses supposedly dallied with the fair siren. One wonders what either Calypso or Ulysses saw in this place, apart from the view, as the narrow stairs lead to a singularly unimpressive and murky hole.

**Ramla Bay** itself is Gozo's biggest golden-sand beach. It has a simple bar in summer, and plenty of space to sun yourself, despite its popularity. North west of Ramla, Għajn Barrani is accessible only by a primitive road which stops at the head of a cliff. After this you have to scramble down: the setting is lovely, however, and the rocks flat and perfect for sunbathing.

Just off the main road from Victoria to Mġarr, **Xewkija** is a rather plain town with an amazing church begun in 1951 and completed 30 years later. Built to a classical design in golden globigerina limestone, it is a typical Gozitan accomplishment, realized by sheer labour and the devotion of the town's 3,500 citizens. Here the **dome** rivals Malta's at Mosta as one of the largest in the world. The parishioners wanted the church so badly that they built it right over the old one, only removing the first when the new building could be used. Some of its features are preserved in a side-chapel.

**Xlendi** is reached by a small road leading south west from Victoria. It is a lovely natural site, well worth the 3-km (2-mile) trip from the island capital, though it can be crowded. On the way, you'll see hilly pastoral scenery and, on the left, a massive wash-house from the knights' time, adorned with the arms of the Order. Xlendi stands at the seaward end of a long and beautifully terraced *wied*, or valley.

The pastel houses of the town are tucked away at the head of a narrow bay protected by two tall rocky promontories. High on the southern side there's a great growth of apartments, but the shore is a favourite spot for swimming. The cliffs opposite are for walkers: follow the main path to its end, through a natural rock garden dotted with wild flowers in winter and spring, and you'll come to an old rock-cut boathouse. With hotels, cafés and restaurants, Xlendi enjoys its status as a favourite excursion haunt, where little shops sell lace, knitwear and other local products.

An adjacent road out of Victoria leads to **Sannat**, a tiny town well-known for its lace-

*There are spectacular clifftop walks near Ta' Ċenċ on Gozo. Xlendi provides a different pleasure amongst its pastel houses.*

making. Just beyond it, the Ta' Ċenċ hotel is built from native stone and discreetly hidden among the trees. Youll find it along a short walk from the dramatic **Ta' Ċenċ** cliffs and the huge new reservoir that is a boon to the neighbouring towns. The rough stony countryside between the hotel and the cliff tops is a good area for finding prehistoric 'cart tracks' (see p.12).

All roads lead from Victoria, and Marsalforn is about 4km (2½ miles) to the north east. On the way you'll see several old windmills and, crowning a peak to the left, a statue of Christ. Once a quiet fishing harbour, **Marsalforn** has become a popular holiday centre for its opportunities for diving, sailing, and swimming off the short, sandy beaches and inviting rock ledges.

Walk or drive west along the coastal tracks to see strange sculpted saltpans, or head inland through rugged country to **Żebbuġ**, which has a traditional church and good views. (You can also take the wider road there from Victoria.)

Ask anybody hereabouts for the house of Sebastian Axiak, a local farmer who turned his hand to sculpting and made a big diorama. He died years ago, but the family is happy to display his creation, a charming potpourri of Christian lore, village scenes and bell-towers from all over the world.

West of Victoria is Gozo's least populated and, some say, prettiest area. The latest part to have been settled, it was once known as the 'desert'. Hikers should aim for one of Gozo's less-visited beauty spots – the gorge of **Wied el-Għasri** – where it meets the sea.

On a side road between Għammar and Għarb is a vast neo-Romanesque church, **Ta' Pinu**, built between 1920-36. The main attraction of this incongruous affair is the miracles connected with it. This was the site of a somewhat run-down chapel (built 1534), which had been cared for by a pious man called Gauci, nicknamed Pinu. On 22 June 1883, a peasant woman, Carmela Grima, heard a mysterious voice urging her to say three *aves*. She heard a similar voice several times, and a friend of hers, Francesco Portelli, admitted he had heard voices too. The two prayed for his desperately ill mother, who recovered miraculously, and from then on the miracles multiplied. Ta' Pinu is still a shrine and place of pilgrimage. A path opposite is lined with marble statues depicting the Stations of the Cross.

Nearby, just outside Għarb, a little museum houses small objects and dioramas made by the pious Portelli and Carmela Grima. To see them, ask the priest at Ta' Pinu, who can arrange to open the museum.

**Għarb** (Arabic for 'west') is the perfect peaceful Gozitan village, with a lovely baroque

*You can visit the Inland Sea on a fisherman's boat or by taking a swim.*

*A focus of pilgrimage, the church of Ta' Pinu and its statues depicting the Stations of the Cross.*

church on its main square, pastel house fronts, a tiny village shop and little else to do but watch the women making lace. The square is decorated with coloured pillars and lights at *festa* time in early July.

Just south of Għarb, take the small road through San Lawrenz down to **Dwejra** for some spectacular sightseeing and bathing. As you descend you'll see a big outcrop in the water which almost entirely blocks the entrance to Qawra Bay. Named General's Rock, it's more often called Fungus Rock after a plant found there and prized by the knights for its curative powers.

The bay below is dominated by Qawra Tower, built in 1651. The road ends near a chapel and an extraordinary rock promontory, where you can walk across a natural arch over the sea. Down a track to the right is the **Inland Sea**, a grandiose name for a saltwater lagoon linked by a natural tunnel to the sea. When it's calm, you can swim through in about

10 minutes. Some boat-houses are open in summer as snack-bars or little shops.

Fast-growing **Nadur**, 5km (3 miles) east of Victoria, is the second largest town in Gozo, and the richest. The people are proud of their church, built by G Bonnici in the 18th century, restored in the 19th, and elaborately decorated. The town is at quite an altitude for Gozo – over 150m (500ft) above sea level (the name Nadur means 'summit' in Arabic).

For isolated rock bathing in a pretty setting, you can take a narrow road north of Nadur, then walk down past orange groves sheltered by bamboo fences to **San Blas**. Another branch of the same road from Nadur takes you to the charming, small fishing harbour of **Daħlet Qorrot**, where boat-houses are carved out of the cliffs. **Qala** is a country town, its windmill is the last one working in Gozo. Further on are quarries which supplied the stone for the Roman Catholic Cathedral of Liverpool.

As in Malta, almost everything is an excursion on Gozo. It's worth hiring a boat for a trip round Gozo and Comino. There are lovely bays, soaring cliffs, and Comino's popular lagoon where you can swim in limpid turquoise waters.

**Strong Medicine**

The plant growing on Fungus Rock which the knights so valued is not actually a fungus at all, but a parasitic species called *Cynomorium coccineum*. Drawing nourishment from the roots of other plants, it pushes up orange-red, leafless spikes. The knights discovered it had haemostatic properties (controlling the flow of blood) and was useful in treating intestinal disorders, a skill for which Malta was notorious almost until modern times. The stuff was thought so precious that anyone found even attempting to raid the rock could be sentenced to death or – a fate scarcely less dire – the galleys.

# What to Do

## Sports

The choice is yours. Malta's climate makes it a paradise for sports and activities. Aware of the latest trend towards healthy exercise, many of the bigger hotels have added tennis and squash courts, gyms, saunas and indoor pools to their range of facilities. Naturally, watersports come first in summer, and the cooler months are just perfect for walking the coastal paths and hills.

### SWIMMING

It's free to swim everywhere except at a few clubs where you can have the benefits of a terrace restaurant, changing rooms and showers. In popular spots you can rent a sunbed or mat and beach umbrella.

There are about a dozen small sandy beaches on Malta, notably Golden Bay, Ġnejna Bay, Paradise Bay and Mellieħa Bay. But even prettier scenery and better snorkelling can be enjoyed at the rocky beach sites, such as Peter's Pool, Marsaskala, Għar Lapsi, around St Paul's Bay and the seaward side of Sliema, though that can be crowded.

On Gozo, the only sizeable stretch of sand is Ramla Bay, with another handful of tiny beaches – or plenty of rocks to swim from – at San Blas, Daħlet Qorrot, Hondoq, Mġarr ix-Xini, Xlendi, the 'Inland Sea' and Marsalforn.

### WATER-SKIING AND PARAGLIDING

You can get a tow and take off at all the main beaches and bigger resort hotels. If you plan to do much water-skiing, try to negotiate a 'package deal' price: paying for lots of single trips is expensive.

### WINDSURFING

As popular here as on any holiday coast, windsurfing is well-organized, with boards for hire at hotels and beaches, and beginners' lessons available. For the experts, international competitions include the Malta to Sicily race in May. The sheltered bays – Mellieħa, St Paul's, Marsamxett, Marsaskala, St Thomas, St George's and Ramla often ripple with coloured sails.

## SCUBA DIVING AND SNORKELLING

The snorkelling possibilities are good everywhere you can swim, and especially off rocky shores, where the water can be wonderfully clear. So bring your masks, snorkels and flippers, or buy or rent them at beach centres.

The Maltese islands can claim some of the world's best diving and, except for a few winter storms, it's an all-year-round sport. You must have a permit from the Department of Health, Merchants Street, Valletta (you'll need a medical certificate, two photos and a logbook to get one). To dive independently from a diving school you must be able to show advanced qualifications.

You'll find licensed schools at St Julian's, St Paul's Bay/Qawra, Marsaskala, Paradise Bay, Valletta and Gzira, on Comino, and at Marsalforn, Xlendi and Xewkija on Gozo. They can give instruction to all levels, and take care of the administrative details as well.

An excellent leaflet (*Malta – Mecca for Divers*) is published by the National Tourist Office, giving addresses, regulations, a guide to prices and a description of main sites.

## BOATING AND SAILING

Malta has a long season of fine sailing weather, and if you don't come in your own boat you can rent anything from a luxury craft to a dinghy here. Marsamxett Harbour is the main centre, with marinas at Ta 'Xbiex and Msida, and also full repair facilities on Manoel Island, where you can find out about berthing and charter. The Valletta Yacht Club, also on

*Following in father's favourite pursuit: children learn fishing at Marsaxlokk.*

Manoel Island, accepts temporary members. Regattas are held from April to November.

Even if you don't sail yourself, be sure to take the opportunity to get afloat. There are countless cruises and excursions to every part of the coast, some in glass-bottomed boats from which to view the underwater scene.

## FISHING

It's free to all and you will not need a licence, but a little politeness goes a long way, so ask the locals whether they mind before you fish from their favourite rock. If you want to go out on a boat, inquire at one of the harbours: Marsaxlokk or St Paul's Bay (and

Mġarr or Marsalforn on Gozo). Spearfishing without a licence is forbidden.

## WALKING

Almost every distant point on the islands is reached by some sort of track, though you may not be happy about one of the reasons – to give access to bird-trappers and hunters. The sign 'RTO' is short for *riservato*, meaning 'private hunting ground'. Wear strong shoes or thick-soled trainers, so as to be comfortable along the rougher tracks and sharp-edged eroded limestone.

Some of the most scenic routes on Malta are the ridges and cliff-top paths of the north and west coast. All of Gozo's coast and hills are well worth exploring. The north-western end has rewards that can be reached only on foot.

## THE MARSA SPORTS CLUB

Situated between Grand Harbour and the airport, this centre has tennis, squash, billiards, a pool, an 18-hole golf course, plus a bar club-house and restaurant. Visitors can join on a weekly basis, or for longer. Horse racing (mostly trotting but also a few flat races) takes place at Marsa racecourse each Sunday from October to May, and stables in the area offer riding facilities.

## OTHER SPORTS

There are indoor bowling centres at Msida and St Julian's, and you might see the traditional Maltese bowls (*bocci*) in the villages. You can go roller-skating at St Julian's, and indulge in archery, table tennis and badminton at the Marsa Club. The strong-swimming locals can be found playing water-polo wherever there's a suitable pool.

Playing, watching, reading and talking about football is a national pastime. Except in high summer, dozens of teams compete in league and cup competitions. International and other important matches take place at the National Stadium at Ta' Qali.

## Shopping

There are few big stores on Malta and you'll probably do most of your buying in small shops and markets. Prices are generally reasonable, and the one quoted is the real price. Haggling is not a way of life here, though it can be worth negotiating terms at outdoor bric-à-brac stalls or at small jeweller's shops.

### BEST BUYS

**Silver**, especially delicate filigree work, is most attractive and enticingly priced. The only problem is choosing from the wonderful displays of Maltese crosses, earrings, necklaces,

*Wise and experienced old hands create intricate bobbin lace in a sunlit Gozitan doorway.*

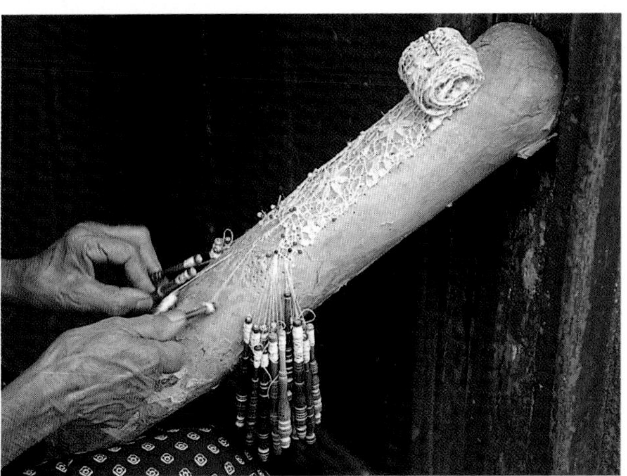

little boats and boxes. The same shapes are also fashioned in gold.

**Lace**, made in Malta and especially on Gozo by women who often sit working in their doorways, is an ideal gift or souvenir – light and unbreakable! Creating the borders for handkerchieves, placemats and tablecloths, it can be fine and intricate. But look carefully before buying, and compare examples: some of the work can be rather rough.

You can see almost every kind of craft practised on the islands at the Crafts Village, Ta' Qali, near Mdina, housed in the buildings of a former airfield. The **glass** makers here mould and blow remarkable shapes in subtle blends of colours – turquoise blue, bottle green and varying shades of brown. This particular style was started by two Englishmen and enthusiastically adopted by local artisans to make ornaments and vases, glasses, decanters and ashtrays. Other glass works can be visited on Manoel Island and near Għarb on Gozo.

Look through the range of **pottery** and **ceramics** – you'll probably find something that appeals to you. Another workshop at Ta' Qali cuts and polishes 'Malta Stone' (good for gifts), a banded brown-and-white calcite, into bookends, ashtrays and souvenirs.

Hand- and machine-knitted **woollens** are on sale in shops and stalls all over the islands. The weather may not be appropriate, but you might find an Aran-style sweater, a pullover or a shawl at a fair price. Feel the wool: it can vary from soft and angora-like to quite hard and prickly.

The crafts centre just across the square from St John's Co-Cathedral concentrates the islands' products in a single display, ranging from original folk art to garish kitsch. The best spots to shop on Gozo are at the Citadel Crafts Centre and in the crafts village at Ta' Dbiegi near San Lawrenz.

Other good buys include locally made cotton swimwear and underwear, jeans, printed and plain T-shirts, and various interesting tea towels.

# Festivals

The Maltese will celebrate at the drop of a hat, and fortunately there are plenty of opportunities. In fact, it is a duty for each parish to mark its saint's day with a joyous *festa*, and since there are 64 parishes in Malta and 14 in Gozo, the calendar is full.

It just so happens that most *festi* fall during the summer months. The main celebrations are usually moved to the weekend following the actual saint's day, but they are preceded by three days of prayer services. Thanksgiving masses are held in the morning, in churches decorated with flowers, huge silver candlesticks and red silk damask hangings. Brass bands parade through town and men carry a statue of the saint in procession through the packed crowds. There's a concert in the main square, and an often excellent fireworks display (generally timed for the Saturday night). Exact dates for the whole year's *festi* can be obtained from the National Tourist Office.

Apart from local festivals, there are a dozen or so fixed national public holidays (see p.127) and one, Good Friday, which is moveable. **Carnival**, the spell of merrymaking before Lent, therefore also moves from year to year but generally falls in late February. Grotesque masks, decorated floats, parties and traditional dances (including the *parata* which commemorates the knights' victory over the Turks in 1565) add up to a five-day feast of frollicking.

**Good Friday** is marked by processions of hooded penitential figures carrying statues of scenes from the Passion, and men and women dressed up as various biblical characters. **Easter Sunday** sees more processions celebrating the risen Christ, and children take their *figolla* (iced marzipan cakes) to be blessed.

The **Commemoration of 7 June 1919** is a national holiday, and later that month is the **Imnarja** folklore festival, held on the Feast of St Peter and St Paul (29 June) in Buskett Gardens.

*The ceiling of Valletta's Manoel Theatre (1731), one of the oldest theatres in the world still in use.*

On 8 September, the feast day for Our Lady of Victories, the celebrations of victory in the two Great Sieges include the **Regatta** in Grand Harbour. Muscular oarsmen battle for prizes and honour amid a bedlam of sirens, horns and cheers (the sailors' turn comes in the **Autumn Races** organized by the Valletta Yacht Club during a week in October). Later in September **Independence Day** is celebrated (21 September).

**Republic Day** on 13 December is marked by a public holiday and parades, music and fireworks, particularly in Vittoriosa. The year's celebrations climax with Christmas – an occasion for family gatherings – and New Year's Eve parties.

## Entertainment

Nightlife is mainly limited to the resort areas – Sliema, St Julian's, and Buġibba/Qawra – where there's plenty of activity. It's mostly quite informal, centred around the handful of discos and the bars and pubs that put on entertainment. And it doesn't go on very late.

### THEATRE AND CONCERTS

Valletta's beautiful Manoel Theatre stages plays in English and Maltese, concerts by the local orchestra and some ballet or opera during a season that lasts from October to May. Visiting international soloists and groups appear there too: they say how much they like its intimate atmosphere and acoustics. In the summer there may be outdoor performances of plays in San Anton Gardens. You can stay informed about schedules by reading *What's On*. Occasional plays and other shows are put on in Gozo's two theatres as well, during the winter months.

## CINEMA

Although you can't expect the latest releases, Sliema and Valletta do have a few cinemas, with the occasional one also in other towns. Gozo's are in Victoria. Films are mostly in English, with a few in Italian. Programmes change often and tend towards the sensational or forgettable.

## NIGHTLIFE

You can go to dinner-dances in many of the big hotels, or a buffet and cabaret combination in St Julian's. Some of the pubs in Paceville put on entertainment, and many bars (both in hotels and out) have live music you can dance to. 'Malta by Night' tours, barbecue-and-folklore evenings, 'Medieval Banquets' and the like have been cooked up as excursions to provide further variety for holidaymakers.

Discos are a magnet to the young. Some are hi-tech with intricate light shows; others are just an open space beneath the stars on summer nights – when they're at their liveliest. Unfortunately for night owls, but luckily for locals who want to sleep, they close early – midnight for most, later for some clubs (all of whom charge an entrance fee).

The palatial Casino, at Dragonara Point, St George's Bay (St Julian's) features roulette, blackjack and slot machines, plus a bar and restaurant. It opens at 8pm and closes in the small hours, depending on the action. Take your passport if you want to go in and join the dedicated or casual gamblers, or even just to look.

# Eating Out

A glance at the market stalls will tell you of the possibilities. The best of Maltese food is full of Mediterranean colour and flavour – juicy tomatoes, bright green and red peppers, squash, salad crops all the year round, and the freshest of fish. Genuine Maltese cooking does exist, though you have to look for it among all the influences from Italy (pasta muscles in everywhere) and Britain (fish and chips and an unfortunate touch of blandness).

It is possible to eat well for a reasonable price, especially simple dishes like fresh *fettucine* in a sauce, or grilled swordfish. Maltese bread, with a crisp brown crust and soft 'holey' inside, is a treat, but white French-style bread and sliced loaves tend to be somewhat tasteless.

The choice of restaurants is vast on Malta, and Gozo has a good selection too. You'll find everything from the most basic, with plastic tables and strip lighting (where it's possible to eat a local pie for next to nothing), right up to an elegant terrace setting overlooking the sea with polished service and superb cuisine. For a change, try Chinese, Japanese, Greek or Turkish food, as authentic as their chefs – from China, Japan, Greece and Turkey – can make it.

Restaurants are classified into four grades by the government. This system generally corresponds to price ranges, though they may not be a reliable guide to quality.

Hours of service are quite conventional: lunch is usually served between noon and 2 or 2.30pm and dinner between 7 and 10pm.

Breakfast in hotels may be continental, 'English' (with a cooked dish) or buffet-style. It's normally included in the room rate, except, paradoxically, in the most expensive places.

*Hors d'oeuvres local style – restaurants serving real Maltese cuisine are quite hard to find.*

## Starters

You'll often see appetizers and hors d'oeuvres listed, as the Italians do, as *antipasti*. They may include slices of local pepper sausage, raw or cooked mixed vegetables, Parma ham (or a similar style) and melon or prawn cocktail. Soups include *kawlata* or *minestra*, which are hearty concoctions of everything in the kitchen garden and more filling than the Italian *minestrone*. *Consommés*, fresh (and tinned) tomato soup and mulligatawny (from India via Britain) feature on many menus. If you like something spicy, look out for fish soups: the best come laden with chunks of different fish and shellfish and laced with garlic and chilli peppers.

## Pasta

There are many Italian restaurants offering a variety of pasta dishes, some of them excellent, and the numerous international restaurants also usually have a pasta section on the menu. You'll see all varieties, from

*The local catch in Victoria's It-Tokk market includes* pixxispada *(swordfish), usually grilled.*

the ubiquitous *spaghetti bolognese* to *vermicelli alle vongole* (with clams). In addition to these, there are some genuine Maltese pasta dishes. *Timpana*, when home-made, is a flaky pastry pie filled with macaroni, minced meat, onion, tomato, aubergine, egg and cheese. The version sold in snack bars cuts down on everything but the pastry and macaroni – it's economical and filling. *Ravjul* is a local version of *ravioli*.

## Fish and Shellfish

Landed that very morning and as fresh as can be, fish is prime fare in Malta – usually simply cooked – grilled, steamed, or fried whole, or *alla Maltese* (with a tomato and green pepper sauce).

*Lampuka* is Malta's 'own' fish, which gathers under offshore floats put out specially for it. The opening of the season (it begins in late August and lasts until November) is a big moment, when the fishermen raise their little triangular flags in salute. A kind of dolphin-fish (nothing to do with dolphins!), *lampuka* is served grilled, casseroled with wine and herbs, in a pie (*torta tal-lampuki*) or fried, then cooked in a pastry shell along with onion, tomatoes, cauliflower, spinach and perhaps olive oil and walnuts.

Octopus, squid (*calamari*) and cuttlefish are often served up as salads, spicy stews, or stuffed. Grilled swordfish (*pix-xispada*) and tuna steaks are good stand-bys. Other fine fish may hide behind unfamiliar names: *dott* (bass) and *ċerna* (grouper) can be excellent. Various types of prawns are popular and lobster, as in most places, is expensive.

## Meat

Carnivores can find a T-bone or a pepper steak on most menus, but it is worth looking for something more typically Maltese such as *braġoli*, a slice of beef rolled round a filling of bacon, breadcrumbs, egg, parsley and a touch of garlic, fried, then simmered in onions and wine.

The islanders will often casserole beef and lamb with potatoes and onions in their homes, and that's what 'roast beef Maltese-style' means on menus. However, most local meat dishes – braised pork, ox tongue in wine sauce and fricassé of meatballs and sweetbreads rarely appear on the menu at all. The only meat dish most people, locals included, used to think of as typically Maltese was *fenek* (rabbit), which was either fried or stewed with wine and garlic. That's now changing, with the growth of interest in national cuisine and the opening of several restaurants offering it.

You'll find good veal *(vitello)* on Italian-style menus, and the chicken is reliable. It's probably the British liking for roast lamb and lamb chops that make them a continuing staple.

## Salads and Vegetables

Good fresh produce is always available. No matter how bad the drought, ingenious irrigation systems trickle water to the terraces and greenhouses. You should find good spinach, courgettes and tomatoes. Baby new potatoes in butter are delicious and so are the chips (French fries) and baked potatoes. Other well-known Maltese staples include stuffed green peppers and succulent aubergines, fried or baked.

## Cheeses

Here you're close enough to the source to get a variety of excellent Italian cheeses – plus other imports from France, Switzerland and Britain. Look out as well for the different kinds of sheep's-milk cheeses (*ġbejna*) made in Malta and Gozo. Mostly small and round, they can be dry and hard, but they are also available in brine and capers, or rolled in black peppercorns. Gozo specializes in goat's-milk cheese (*ġbejniet*), which also comes in the form of roundels.

## Desserts and Fruit

The Maltese have a distinctly sweet tooth, so there's plenty of Italian-style ice-cream in many flavours, and cake shops and restaurants provide *semifreddo* ice-cream cake confections. Various types of *gâteaux* and *torte* (cakes and tarts) are on many menus. The best are mouth-watering but some versions on tourist menus can be dry and artificial-tasting.

Soft *ricotta* cheese is sometimes used in sweet cheesecakes with fruit or combined with chocolate, cherries, sugar and almonds to fill little cornets called *kannoli tar-rikotta. Helwa tat-tork* is ultra sweet, made from sesame flour.

Festivals bring their own special sweet things. At Easter you'll see *figolli* in the shops, iced almond-lemon biscuits cut in various shapes. *Prinjolata* is a combination of sponge fingers, butter cream and almonds or pinenuts, and decorated with chocolate and cherries. And no *festa* is complete without the ubiquitous almond, nougat and doughnut stalls.

Fresh fruit makes an ideal dessert: peaches, plums, apricots and figs in summer, then melons, followed by oranges and tangerines in winter. The strawberry season lasts longer and longer, with new varieties and techniques developed for

*A red pillar-box and Queen Victoria may remind you of Britain. The pleasure of sitting in an open-air café probably won't.*

the export business. And if you haven't yet tried prickly pears now's your chance, but beware of the tiny spines that cover them. Get them on your hands, or worse, in your mouth, and you'll itch for hours. Experts say they don't stick into you when they're wet with the morning dew!

## Snacks

It's part of the local way of life to pick up a sandwich, pie or meat-filled pasty at a tiny snack bar or a stall in the street. *Pastizzi* or *qassata,* various flaky pastry turn-overs or pies with a filling of *ricotta*, peas and onion, or anchovies are especially popular. In local bars you'll see customers enjoying a plate of snails with their beer.

## Drinks and Wines

The fruit juices are excellent, especially the fresh ones, of course, but also the cartons you see everywhere. Try the pear, peach, apricot, and exotic mixtures. The usual soft drinks are available: a local brand called *Kinnie* is rather like an orange-flavoured cola. Maltese beer and lager are good and inexpensive: imports tend to cost about twice as much.

Imported fine or ordinary wines can be found both in stores and on restaurant lists, but Malta itself produces some very drinkable wines sold for a much lower price. The reds are quite full-bodied, although the cheaper kind can be rather acidic. Four famous brands are *Marsovin Special Reserve*, *Lachryma Vitis*, *Farmers* and *Festa*. Look out for *La Valette* and four- or five-year-old *Marsovin Cabernet Sauvignon.*

The same four brand names appear on white wines. They are mostly dry and fruity, and refreshing when well chilled. *Sauternes*, not surprisingly, are very sweet. The more respectable of Gozo's wines include Velson's red and white. The Ġgantija wines, both red and white, are sweeter. Watch out for the high alcohol content of some of the local wines. Also beware of the mild to drastic laxative effect that drinking too much of them can have.

# BLUEPRINT for a Perfect Trip

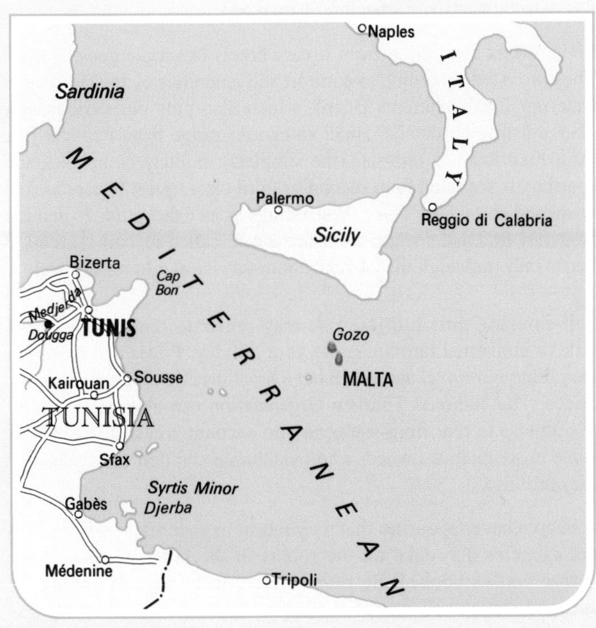

# An A–Z Summary of Practical Information

## A

**ACCOMMODATION** (See also YOUTH HOSTELS, and RECOMMENDED HOTELS beginning on p.65)

Malta offers everything from luxury hotels to simple guest houses. They are rated according to comfort and amenities by the Hotels and Catering Establishments Board, which also puts out various brochures listing all details. Hotel categories range from five-star (the most luxurious) to one-star (the simplest); holiday complexes and aparthotels are rated first, second or third class; guest houses as first or second class. Don't take these ratings as an exact guide to quality. You may find that a warm welcome at a so-called second-class guest house may outweigh the 24-hour room service at a five-star hotel.

**Self-catering possibilities**. You may prefer to rent an apartment, villa or converted farmhouse for your holiday. Prices and amenities vary, but your travel agent will have brochures detailing choices and prices. The National Tourism Organization can also provide lists. It's unwise to rent from someone you encounter casually: there are some unscrupulous owners who overcharge and don't provide what they promise.

People have favourites that they return to year after year, and travel agencies may take all the rooms in the hotel of your choice before you've booked. So reserve early to be sure of getting the accommodation you want.

## AIRPORT

The Maltese islands are served by Luqa Airport, some 6km (4 miles) south of Valletta, a driving time of about 15 minutes. The airport can take jumbo jets, and is used by Air Malta and some of the other international airlines. Customs formalities are fairly simple, with the usual red and green channels. There's a currency-exchange counter open 24 hours a day. The airport has an air-conditioned restaurant, a snack bar, bookstall and car hire desks. The duty-free shop sells tobacco, perfume, wines and spirits – and you can also buy on arrival. An Air Malta information counter helps with inquiries and problems. The airport post office is open Monday to Saturday, 7am to 7pm.

The bus stop for Valletta is a two-minute walk from the terminal building. Some hotels run an airport minibus service, and taxis are available.

There's no airport on Gozo, though there is a helicopter link in summer (see PUBLIC TRANSPORT – FERRIES for how to get to Gozo).

*Note*: Summer travellers are advised to reach the airport in good time for their return flight. It is not unknown for flights to be overbooked.

Flight inquiries: tel. 243455
243458
242876

# B

## BICYCLE HIRE

Cycling can be tiring under the summer sun, but the islands' reasonably flat terrain and short distances are points in favour. Cycles can be rented for relatively little, and you can avoid traffic jams and parking problems. For further details, consult the Tourist Organization (see TOURIST INFORMATION OFFICES).

## CAMPING

There are no organized campsites on Malta or Gozo.

## CAR HIRE (See also DRIVING)

Major international car-hire firms operate in Malta, some with desks at the airport. There are also dozens of small companies, some reliable, others less so. Terms are reasonable, and most visitors prefer hiring to bringing their own cars. However, in peak holiday periods early booking is advisable. The smaller firms may offer inadequate cars: insist on a recent model and check the tyres and general condition. Full insurance cover is recommended. It is not the universal custom to deliver the car with a full tank of petrol: you may need to buy some as soon as you get it.

To hire a car you need a valid driving licence, and some companies may ask to see your passport. Most agencies set a minimum age of 25 for car hire. Reputable firms accept major credit cards as payment, though some may ask for a cash deposit. The rate on page 125 includes tax and third-party insurance. Full cover will cost extra.

And, before you set off, don't forget to DRIVE ON THE LEFT.

**Chauffeur-driven cars**. This way of sightseeing is more comfortable than driving yourself on the rather difficult roads – if you can afford it. The charge per hour is high. Some garages impose a minimum rental period of eight hours. Taxis can also be hired by the hour, half-day or day, with prices ranging wildly according to your bargaining skills.

## CHILDREN'S MALTA

There aren't very many special attractions for children, but they'll be happy all the same, especially on the beaches. The easy, sandy ones are fine for all ages, though you should keep an eye on very young children and toddlers, as there is not much in the way of lifeguard services. Rocky shores are good for older children to swim, snorkel or sail from.

For a change, the young can enjoy screaming down the water-slides at the Splash Park, Bahar ic-Cagħaq, or visiting Popeye Village.

The *festi*, religious festivals, are even more fun for children than for adults. They happen at weekends all summer long (tourist information offices can give you a list of where and when). There are parades, perhaps little fairs, and on Saturday evenings the fireworks can be spectacular. Good displays to watch include the St George festival in Qormi and the St Nicholas festival in Siggiewi, both in late June, and the mid-August festival in Victoria, Gozo.

Children might like the *Imnarja*, or folklore festival, in Buskett Gardens. Also in late June, just after the folklore festival, there's a donkey race at nearby Rabat. More donkey and horse races are held in July, for the feast of St George in Victoria, Gozo, and in August, around the feast of the Assumption, on both islands. Carnival parades take place in February. The regatta – boat races to celebrate Our Lady of Victories – is held on 8 September in Valletta's Grand Harbour.

In St Anton Gardens, Malta, the mini-zoo has a small collection of a few animals and birds.

**Baby-sitting** services are listed in the local papers and in the *What's On* guide.

## CLIMATE

Malta has a typical Mediterranean climate with hot, dry summers and mild, humid winters. Even in winter you can expect a few hours of sunshine most days. The sea has warmed up by May and stays pleasant for swimming until October or even November. In May and from about mid-September to mid-October, the *sirocco* blows in from North Africa, raising the humidity. Sea breezes moderate the heat of summer.

Trees and plants flower early on the island: you'll see 'spring' blossoms from December to March. After that, temperatures climb quickly, and the landscape takes on its characteristic parched appearance. Summer is the main tourist season, but increasing numbers of people are taking advantage of lower winter prices to enjoy a break from cold northern Europe.

| | J | F | M | A | M | J | J | A | S | O | N | D |
|---|---|---|---|---|---|---|---|---|---|---|---|---|
| Air temperature | | | | | | | | | | | | |
| Average daily °F | 58 | 59 | 61 | 65 | 71 | 79 | 84 | 85 | 81 | 75 | 67 | 61 |
| maximum* °C | 14 | 15 | 16 | 18 | 22 | 26 | 29 | 29 | 27 | 24 | 22 | 16 |
| Average daily °F | 50 | 51 | 52 | 56 | 61 | 67 | 72 | 73 | 71 | 66 | 60 | 54 |
| minimum* °C | 10 | 10 | 11 | 13 | 16 | 19 | 22 | 23 | 22 | 19 | 16 | 12 |
| Water temperature | | | | | | | | | | | | |
| °F | 58 | 58 | 58 | 59 | 64 | 70 | 75 | 78 | 77 | 74 | 67 | 61 |
| °C | 14 | 14 | 14 | 15 | 18 | 21 | 24 | 26 | 25 | 23 | 19 | 16 |

* Maximum temperatures are measured in the early afternoon, minimum temperatures just before sunrise.

## CLOTHING

Light and loose cotton clothing is the best daytime wear for the hot summer. Everyone should have a hat or scarf for protection from the sun, and comfortable shoes or sandals for sightseeing.

The heat, however, doesn't mean you can go around half-dressed. The Maltese disapprove of unseemly dress in public places and beachwear away from the beach. Brief shorts, miniskirts, low-cut or shoulder-baring dresses are prohibited for visiting churches. Women may be handed a scarf to cover their shoulders.

Although bikinis are a common sight on beaches, it is illegal to appear topless or nude, and you risk a fine or worse if you try.

In the evening certain luxury hotels and the Casino require men to wear a jacket and tie, and women may need something dressy. Take a jersey or a wrap for cooler evenings. In winter, pack a light jacket, sweater, raincoat and umbrella.

## COMPLAINTS

If things go wrong, try complaining first to the owner or manager of the establishment. The friendly Maltese invariably try to set things right when you explain your problem. If you are still not satisfied, you can then go to the National Tourist Organization (see Tourist Information Offices), or call their special number, 245615, where visitors can lodge complaints. This number is staffed during office hours, but at all other times a recording machine registers calls.

If your problem is bad merchandise or car repairs, complain at once to the merchant or car-hire firm. If this fails, go to the National Tourist Organization. Complaints made to the police will usually be referred back to the Tourist Organization or the Hotels and Catering Establishments Board.

## CRIME

Malta is still relatively crime-free compared with the rest of the world, and tourists are safe almost anywhere, but theft is sadly on the increase. It is wise to take the usual precautions. Put your valuables in the hotel safe or, if you've rented a flat, don't leave them in a conspicuous place. Lock your car as a matter of course. Any loss or theft should be reported immediately to the nearest police station, and, if it happened at a hotel, to the hotel management.

The possession, use and distribution of drugs are all considered criminal offences, punishable by fines and/or a prison sentence.

## CUSTOMS and ENTRY FORMALITIES

For a stay of up to three months, a valid passport is sufficient for most visitors.

Here's what you can take into Malta duty free and, when returning home, into your own country:

| **Into**: | Cigarettes | | Cigars | | Tobacco | Spirits | | Wine |
|---|---|---|---|---|---|---|---|---|
| Malta | 200 or 250g of other tobacco products* | | | | | 1 l | or | 1 l |
| Australia | 200 | or | 250 g | or | 250 g | 1 l | and | 1 l |
| Canada | 200 | or | 50 | or | 900 g | 1.1 l | or | 1.1 l |
| Eire | 200 | and | 50 | or | 250 g | 1 l | and | 2 l |
| N. Zealand | 200 | or | 50 | or | 250 g | 1.1 l | and | 4.5 l |
| S. Africa | 400 | and | 50 | and | 250 g | 1 l | and | 2 l |
| UK | 200 | or | 50 | or | 250 g | 1 l | and | 2 l |
| USA | 200 | and | 100 | and | ** | 1 l | or | 1 l |

* of which not more than 50 g in loose tobacco
** a reasonable quantity

**Currency restrictions**. There's no limit on how much foreign currency a non-resident may bring into Malta (large amounts must be declared upon arrival), but you are entitled to import only Lm 50 in local currency. Visitors may export a maximum of Lm 25 in local currency, plus any remaining foreign currency of the sum they bought in and declared to customs upon arrival.

## D

### DRIVING

If you're going to the trouble of taking your car to Malta, you'll need:

• your national driving licence
• car registration papers
• insurance coverage (the most common formula for this is the Green Card, an extension to your regular insurance that makes it valid abroad).

Though there are practically no standard equipment requirements on Malta or Gozo, it is safe policy to use seat belts and bring a red warning triangle for use in emergencies.

**Driving conditions**. The rules in general follow the United Kingdom: drive on the left, overtake on the right; at roundabouts give way to cars coming from the right.

Speed limits are theoretically 40kph (25mph) in built-up areas, 64kph (40mph) on the larger open roads.

The best policy for visitors is to drive defensively, giving a wide berth to lorries and buses, or precedence to aggressive-looking vehicles. Driving in Malta, and especially on Gozo, can be a trial for a newcomer used to order.

In the centre of Valletta many streets are closed to cars, others are one-way, and the rest are usually clogged.

**Road conditions**. There are a few stretches of road big enough for four lanes. Both Malta's and Gozo's main routes, though not always in good repair, are usually wide enough to accommodate two or three vehicles abreast. The roads often have potholes, sometimes repaired by hot tar and an amalgam of stones plus a fine dust topping.

**Distance**

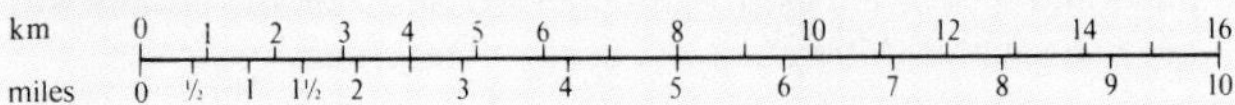


**Fluid measures**

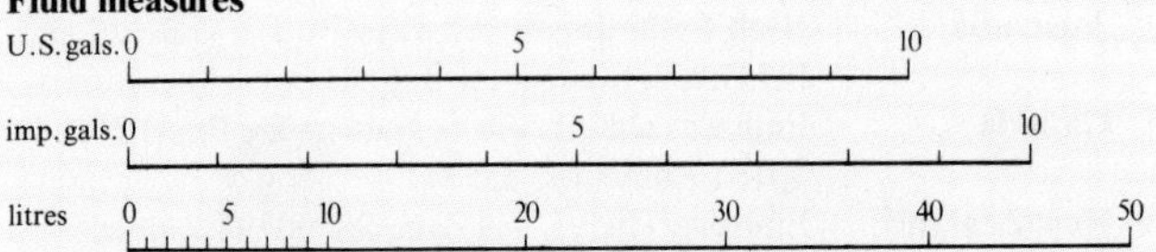


**Parking**. Fines for illegal parking are enforced. Be absolutely sure not to block anyone, or an exit. There are no parking meters. If you put your car in a car park, give the attendant a small tip when you leave.

**Traffic police**. You don't often see them, but they do patrol in cars or on motorcycles. You might occasionally see them stopping vehicles for safety or identity checks.

**Fuel and oil**. Fuel is available in super (98 octane), unleaded and diesel. Service stations open 6.30am-6pm, but close on Sundays and holidays, so be sure not to run low on Saturday night.

**Breakdowns**. Towing and on-the-spot repairs are made by local garages, and spare parts can usually be found for most common makes of car. Malta's mechanics are skilled, as evidenced by all the 40-year-old cars and buses still going strong. If you're renting your car, first call the hire firm, who should send help within the hour.

**Accidents**. In case of an accident, call the police immediately (dial 191). It is wise not to move your vehicle until they arrive, since accident claims are not usually settled unless the police make a report on the spot.

E

## ELECTRIC CURRENT

Electric supply is 240 volts 50 cycle AC. Three-pronged British-type plugs and sockets are used. Australian and New Zealand visitors will need an adaptor, Americans will need a transformer.

## EMBASSIES and HIGH COMMISSIONS

**Australia**: High Commission, Airways House, Gaiety Lane, PO Box 8, Sliema; tel. 338201/5.

**Canada**: Embassy (Italy), Via G. Battista De Rossi 27, 00161 Rome; tel. 855341.

**New Zealand**: Embassy (Italy), Via Zara, 28, 00198 Rome; tel. 4402928.

**UK**: High Commission, 7 St Anne Street, Floriana; tel. 233134/8.

**USA**: Embassy, Development House, St Anne Street, Floriana; tel 623653/620424/623216.

## EMERGENCIES

In case of accident or other emergencies, phone:

Police **191** Ambulance **196** Fire **199**

For traffic accidents, see DRIVING.

## GETTING TO MALTA

Considering the wide variety of fares and regulations and the choice of ways to go, you'll be well-advised to consult a reliable travel agent. That way you have the best chance of meeting your timetable and budget.

**BY AIR**. There are direct flights to Malta's Luqa Airport (see also p.107) from many European cities and several cities in North Africa. Travellers from elsewhere will normally have to fly to a European capital for connecting flights to Malta. Flying time from the UK is about three hours 15 minutes.

Ask about lower fares for children, youths, students and senior citizens, excursions and night flights, as well as inclusive holidays.

**BY RAIL OR ROAD**. If you have the time and plan your journey carefully, the trip by **train** can be enjoyable. Travellers from northern Europe will have to change trains at least once, either in Milan or Rome. Be sure to make advance reservations if you want a sleeping car or couchette.

Discounted train fares are available to senior citizens, youths, children and groups. Travel agencies can give you details.

If you are taking your **car** south to Malta, you can travel right across Europe by motorway but you'll have to pay a toll on motorway routes in France, Switzerland and Italy, and if you use one of the tunnels through the Alps. Putting your car on a train is expensive, but saves on wear and tear, fuel and tolls.

**FERRIES** to Malta run from Naples, Reggio di Calabria, and Catania and Syracuse in Sicily. All carry both cars and passengers. In addition, a fast catamaran carries passengers only between Malta and several Sicilian ports.

## GUIDES

The National Tourist Organization (see TOURIST INFORMATION OFFICES) can provide you with qualified official guides, who must wear an identification tag issued by the Ministry of Tourism, showing their name, licence number and a photograph. Your hotel can also find a guide for you. Tipping is not included in the price of an excursion.

## HEALTH and MEDICAL CARE

In the heat of summer, as in many similar climates, newcomers may contract 'tourist's tummy', often due to fatigue, too much sun and a change of diet. Food and drink are quite safe, but be sure fresh fruit and vegetables are washed.

The water is generally safe for drinking, but it can be unpalatable. Do not drink water from fountains. Water in hotels and homes comes straight from the 'mains', and is therefore safe. Most mineral water is imported. The local brand, slightly bubbly, is *San Michele*.

The local wine can be excellent but the cheapest varieties may have potent laxative effects. If gastro-intestinal or other problems last more than a day or two, consult a doctor.

Beware of the sun, which is very powerful in the summer months. Start with a sunscreen or total-block cream at first and build up a tan gradually in small doses. The occasional salt tablet doesn't do any harm when you're perspiring a lot.

There are plenty of insects in country areas, particularly on Gozo, and in the hottest part of summer. Several sprays are available in the shops if they bother you. Tiny, almost invisible flies can leave itching bites; for these, use the insect repellent and itch-remedy creams obtainable at the pharmacy. The same goes for mosquitoes. If you have mosquitoes in the room, buy an inexpensive coil called 'moon tiger', which smoulders all night and keeps them away. Even more effective (and more expensive) is the electric version of this. Both can be purchased from chemists.

**Insurance**. Malta has a reciprocal agreement with the United Kingdom (and certain other countries) providing nearly the same free health care that the British National Health Service offers. But if you come from elsewhere, make sure your health insurance policy covers accident or illness while on holiday.

**Treatment**. You may not get served in the hospital on silver platters, as did the knights of the Order of St John, but medical equipment and treatment are usually of a reasonable standard. General practitioners will be well qualified.

If you need a doctor urgently, your hotel will help you find one; otherwise, the chemist can be of assistance. In an emergency, you can dial 196 on both Malta and Gozo, or:

Malta, St Luke's Hospital (Gwardamanġa); tel. 241251.

Gozo, Craig Hospital (Għajn Qatet Street, Victoria); tel. 556851.

**Pharmacies**. Clearly marked 'Chemist' or 'Pharmacy', these are usually open during normal working and shopping hours. Duty pharmacies are listed in the local weekend papers.

## HITCH-HIKING

It is permitted, though not common. If you do so, obey the normal common-sense rules, but it is much better to use the cheap and perfectly adequate bus service.



## LANGUAGE

You can get along fine if you speak English, since nearly every Maltese has a good command of it, and many speak Italian as well. However, the first language here is *Malti* – Maltese, which is both fascinating and quite incomprehensible to most foreigners. The pronunciation is especially difficult. Here is a key to some of the trickier consonants:

| | | |
|---|---|---|
| **ċ** | – | like *ch* in *ch*ild |
| **g** | – | as in *g*ood |
| **ġ** | – | like *j* in *j*ob |
| **għ** | – | silent, unless at the end of a word (*h* like in *h*ello) |
| **h** | – | silent, unless at the end of a word (*h* like in *h*ello) |
| **ħ** | – | *h* |
| **j** | – | like *y* in *y*ear; **aj** like *igh* in h*igh*; **ej** like *ay* in s*ay* |
| **q** | – | almost silent – like a very faint *kh*-sound; a bit like cockney glottal stop 'ain't i*t*' |
| **x** | – | like *sh* in *sh*op |
| **z** | – | *ts* |
| **ż** | – | *z* |

**A few everyday expressions**:

| | Maltese | pronunciation |
|---|---|---|
| good morning | **bonġu** | BON-joo |
| good evening | **bonswa** | BON-swah |
| yes | **iva** | EE-vah |
| no | **le** | leh |
| please | **jek jogħġbok** | yehek YOJ-bok |
| thank you | **grazzi** | GRAHT-see |
| excuse me | **skużi** | SKOO-zee |
| Where is ...? | **Fejn hu ...?** | fayn oo |
| right | **lemin** | LEH-meen |
| left | **xellug** | shehl-LOOG |
| straight ahead | **dritt il-quddiem** | drit il-KHOOD-dee-ehm |
| How much? | **Kemm?** | kehm |

**Ta'** means 'the place of'

**Numbers**

| | | |
|---|---|---|
| 0 | **Xejn** | shayn |
| 1 | **Wieħed** | WEE-hehd |
| 2 | **Tnejn** | tnayn |
| 3 | **Tlieta** | TLEE-tah |

| | | |
|---|---|---|
| 4 | **Erbgħa** | EHR-bah |
| 5 | **Ħamsa** | Hum-sah |
| 6 | **Sitta** | SIT-tah |
| 7 | **Sebgħa** | SEH-bah |
| 8 | **Tmienja** | TMEE-ehn-yah |
| 9 | **Disgħa** | DIS-sah |
| 10 | **Għaxra** | AHSH-rah |

For the most common town and site names, see under PLACE NAMES.

## LAUNDRY and DRY-CLEANING

There are ample laundry and dry-cleaning services on both Malta and Gozo, and Malta has some self-service launderettes accessible to tourists during normal business hours. Laundry service takes about three days, as does dry-cleaning. There are express one-day services, however, and top hotels offer both regular and same-day service, but same-day costs a lot more than the regular.

## LOST PROPERTY

Check first where you think you lost the object; the Maltese people are, in general, scrupulously honest about other people's property. If you can't find the object, try at the nearest police station.

**Lost children**. Don't let young children out of your sight in crowded places (like the swarming main streets of Valletta). If a child is really missing, report it immediately to the police.

## MAPS

The tourist offices in Valletta and Victoria, Gozo, hand out a very basic map, which might also be available from your hotel. Otherwise, there's a good choice of maps at bookshops, hotel news-stands, and the like.

## MEETING AND GREETING PEOPLE

To help you meet the Maltese there are no 'official' organizations, but you really need no such help. The people are proud and dignified, yet kind and friendly. If you want to enter into conversation, discuss the beauties of their islands. They may invite a complete stranger round for a drink, or to share tea or coffee in a hotel or café. Whenever problems arise, whoever is around will try sincerely to help, whether locating an address, finding a telephone or getting your car repaired. In shops or restaurants, on guided tours, at the beach or pool, it is easy to meet the Maltese. Young people also mix and meet at the many discos.

The islanders have the casual Mediterranean way of looking at things, and 'tomorrow' or 'later this afternoon' is just as good as 'right now' for getting things done. So be insistent if you really have to, while trying not to hurry them too much. They have a strict Catholic upbringing, and are usually very polite. They treat each other and strangers with courtesy, and expect the same in return.

Nobody is going to ask you to speak a word of Maltese, but you will get amused and happy smiles if you try out *bonġu* ('good morning') and *bonswa* ('good evening'), *skużi* ('excuse me'), pronounced just like the Italian) and *grazzi* ('thank you' almost like Italian). See also LANGUAGE.

## MONEY MATTERS

**Currency**. The Maltese pound is divided into 100 cents (¢), the cent into 10 mils (m). Within the country, the pound is referred to as *Lira,* plural *Liri* (abbreviated Lm)

*Notes*: Lm 2, 5, 10 and 20.

*Coins*: 2m, 3m and 5m and 1¢, 2¢, 5¢, 10¢, 25¢, 50¢ and Lm 1.

Inflation has eroded the usefulness of the mil coins: you won't usually be asked for them, but you might get some in change.

Malta's gold and silver proof and brilliant uncirculated coins for collectors are sold at the Malta Coins Distribution Centre, Central Bank of Malta, Castile Place, Valletta, at the issue price. Coins whose issue is closed can be bought from coin dealers. To take more than just a few souvenir coins out of Malta, you'll need a permit from the Central Bank of Malta.

For currency restrictions, see under CUSTOMS AND ENTRY REGULATIONS.

**Banking hours**. In summer, hours are generally 8am-12 noon, Monday-Friday, (until 11.30am on Saturdays); in winter, banks open and close half an hour later. Some bank branches in main centres have foreign-exchange desks open in the afternoons, from 4-7pm (3-6pm in winter).

On Saturdays, banks will change foreign cash up to the value of Lm 100 for tourists. Many hotels give low rates of exchange for **traveller's cheques**, so it's usually better to go to a bank. You'll need your passport when cashing traveller's cheques. **Credit cards** are widely accepted by major shops, hotels and restaurants in the bigger towns. Usually, the symbols of the cards accepted are on display. In shops, pay with Maltese currency or credit cards, unless they are advertising a special high rate for your foreign currency.

**Prices** are reasonable when compared with the big continental cities. Food is inexpensive. Handicrafts (weaving, lace, knitting, pottery, glass, etc) are good buys (see Shopping, p.93). Prices are usually fixed, but you can try your bargaining skills at market stalls, street stands and some smaller jewellers selling souvenirs. Some prices are listed on page 125 as a guide.



## NEWSPAPERS and MAGAZINES

All the British dailies and the *International Herald Tribune* are usually available in the afternoon of the day of publication (the next day on Gozo) at most news-stands. There is one English-language daily published in Malta, *The Times*, and one weekly, *The Sunday Times*.

The small fortnightly *What's On* guide gives a vast amount of information on everything from restaurants and cinemas to tips for the tourist.

## OPENING HOURS

Everything closes up for a few hours around lunchtime. The summer heat can be unbearable; so do as the locals do – relax until the cool of late afternoon.

Hours of opening vary widely according to the establishment, whether government or private, the day of the week, and the time of year. The following is an indication of the general rules. (See also under COMMUNICATIONS and MONEY MATTERS.)

**Government offices**. Winter (1 October-15 June): 7.45am-12.30pm and 1.15-5.15pm Monday-Friday. Summer: 7.30am-1.30pm Monday-Friday.

**Offices and Businesses**. 8.30 or 9am-1 or 1.30pm and 2.30-5.30 or 6pm, Monday-Friday. A few operate on Saturday mornings. Most head or managing offices follow Government schedules.

**Shopping hours** are generally from 9am-7pm with a one- to three-hour break for lunch (usually closer to three), Monday to Saturday. Some establishments remain open during lunch, and some stay open until 8pm on Saturdays.

The open-air market in Merchants Street, Valletta, operates until about noon, Monday to Saturday. On Sundays, a much larger morning market attracts crowds to St James Ditch just outside the walls of Valletta, a stone's throw from the bus terminus.

**Museums**. Most museums and sites are state-run and have fairly uniform hours. Winter (1 October-15 June): 8.15am-5pm Monday-Saturday, 8.15am-4.15pm on Sundays. Summer: 7.45am-2pm including Sundays. Closed on public holidays. In Gozo, museums are open 8.30am-4.30pm Monday-Saturday in winter, 8.30am-6.30 or 7pm in summer. At the Hypogeum, Paola, visitor numbers are restricted: if you don't go with a tour, you may have to wait at the site to join a group to go in.

**Mdina Cathedral Museum**. 9am-1pm and 1.30-4.30pm (5pm in summer). Closed Sundays and holidays.

**Manoel Theatre**. 10.45am and 11.30am tours Monday to Friday.

**National War Museum**, Fort St Elmo, times as for state museums.

**War Rooms**, Lascaris Bastion, 9am-12.30pm Monday, Wednesday, Friday.

**St. John's Co-Cathedral**. 9am-1pm and 3-5.30pm Monday-Friday; 9.30am-1pm and 3.30-5pm on Saturday. The museum and oratory shut one hour earlier Monday-Friday, at lunchtime on Saturday. All are shut on Sundays.

**The Malta Experience**, Mediterranean Conference Centre: shows at 10.30am, noon, 1.30pm, 3pm, 4pm; Saturday 11am, 12 noon. Closed Sunday.

**Gozo Heritage**, Mġarr Road: shows 10am-4pm Monday-Saturday. Closed Sunday.

**The Mdina Experience**, 7 Mesquita Square: shows 10am-4pm Monday-Saturday. Closed Sunday.



## PHOTOGRAPHY

There are plenty of subjects to appeal to the amateur or professional – spectacular views where cliffs of pastel-coloured rock tumble into the dark blue or turquoise sea, colourful fishing boats, craftspeople at work, the gold of sunset on ancient walls and the special challenge of underwater photography. The deep shadows of alleyways and the fierce light of midday at prehistoric sites are a severe test.

Most well-known film brands are available, but not everywhere. Valletta has several good photography shops. You may have trouble buying 35-mm black and white film or especially fast film, but major brands of colour print and transparency film are easy to find.

Fast black-and-white development is rare. Colour print film is processed the same day on weekdays.

The airport's X-ray machine does not spoil normal film, but for safety's sake, put it in a bag to be checked separately.

Video tape is readily available.

## **PLACE NAMES** (See also LANGUAGE)

The Maltese like to hear at least their town names pronounced properly. So here's a list of the main sites mentioned in this book.

| | |
|---|---|
| Birżebbuġa | beer-zeeb-BOO-jah |
| Borġ in-Nadur | borj in nah-DOOR |
| Buġibba | Boo-JIB-ba |
| Ġgantija | J'GAHN-tee-yah |
| Għar Dalam | ahr DAH-lam |
| Għar Ħassan | ahr hahs-SAHN |
| Għar Lapsi | ahr LAHP-see |
| Għarb | ahrb |
| Ħaġar Qim | hah-jahr-khEEM |
| Marsamxett | mahr-sahm-SHEHTT |
| Marsaxlokk | mahr-sash-LOKK |
| Mdina | im-DEE-nah |
| Mġarr | im-JAHRR |
| Naxxar | NAHS-shahr |
| Qala | khAH-lah |
| Qawra | khOW-rah |
| Qormi | khOHR-mee |
| Siġġiewi | SEEJ-jee-eh-wee |
| Tarxien | TAHR-sheen |
| Xagħra | SHAH-rah |
| Xlendi | SHLEHN-dee |
| Żebbuġ | ZEHB-booj |
| Żejtun | ZAY-toon |

## PLANNING YOUR BUDGET

To give you an idea of what to expect, here is a list of average prices in Malta Liri (Lm). They can only be approximate, especially where competing prices prevail (eg car hire, souvenirs, watersports).

**Accommodation**. Per person, per night, with breakfast (except 5-star). 5-star Lm 28, 4-star Lm 14, 3-star Lm 10, 2-star Lm 8, 1-star Lm 6. Aparthotels and similar: Lm 10 to Lm 5, depending on quality and facilities. Guesthouses: Lm 5-10.

**Airport transfer**. Taxi to Valletta, meter fare Lm 4.50.

**Car hire**. Officially the daily tariff is Lm 7 irrespective of make of car but excluding petrol. Last-minute bookings in summer may exceed this: out-of-season rates and advance reservations made before arrival can be less.

**Ferry to Gozo**. From Ċirkewwa to Mġarr, return, adults Lm 1.50, children 75¢, Lm 3.50 per car. From Sa Maison Pier, Pietà, fares are slightly higher.

**Food and drinks**. Set meal (tourist menu) in medium-priced restaurant Lm 2-3, bottle of local wine from Lm 1.20, soft drinks 20¢, coffee 20¢, beer 25¢.

**Guides**. Up to 11 people: 4 hours Lm 5, 8 hours Lm 7. Both rates must be topped with a free lunch for the guide or Lm 2 as compensation for lunch.

**Shopping**. Beef, fresh from Lm 3 per kg (2lb), frozen from Lm 1.20 per kg (2lb), chicken (frozen) Lm 1 per kg (2lb), potatoes 15¢ per kg (2lb), loaf of bread 13¢ for 750g (1lb 8oz), butter 20¢ for 227g (8oz), milk 12¢ per bottle, local wine 30¢-Lm 1.30 per bottle, whisky/gin Lm 5 per bottle.

**Souvenirs**. Set of three Maltese lace placemats Lm 3.95-8.50, silver cufflinks with Maltese cross Lm 5-6, gold filigree brooch Lm 20, silver filigree brooch Lm 4-8.

**Watersports**. *Rowing boat* Lm 2 per hour; *sailing dinghy* Lm 5-10 for two hours, *windsurfer* Lm 2.50 per hour, *water-skiing* Lm 5 for 10-minute lesson (or Lm 2.50 every 5 minutes), *scuba diving* Lm 10-11 per dive.

## POLICE

Most towns have a police station, clearly marked. Some stations are not manned around the clock. All police officers, whether watching traffic or helping a tourist find the way, are dressed in casual blue cotton uniforms in summer, black uniforms in winter, with visored hats. Don't hesitate to approach them: they are helpful and friendly.

Always contact the police immediately in case of a car accident (see under DRIVING). In an emergency, call the police on 191.

## POST OFFICES

The postal service is generally quite efficient in Malta. The General Post Office at Auberge d'Italie in Merchants Street, Valletta keeps the following hours:

*Summer* (16 June-30 September): 7.30am-6pm Monday-Saturday.

*Winter*: 8am-6.30pm Monday-Saturday.

Branch post offices are open 7.30am-12.45pm Monday-Saturday all year round.

The main branch post office on Gozo is at 129 Republic (Racecourse) Street, Victoria. Hours are the same as Malta's.

Stamps may also be bought at most hotels, some tobacconists and some shops that sell postcards. Mailboxes are painted red.

**Poste Restante (general delivery)**. If you wish to have your mail sent to you c/o Poste Restante, you should write ahead of time to warn the post office (address the letter to the Postmaster General, General Post Office, Valletta, Malta).When going to collect your mail, you will need proof of identity, or if you are sending someone to collect it for you, you will need to give them written authorisation.

**Telegrams**. You can send telegrams from Telemalta in St John's Square, Valletta, 8am-6.30pm Monday-Saturday (except holidays), from Luqa Airport every day 7am-7pm or from the Main Telegraph Office (open 24 hours a day), St George's Road, St Julian's.

There is no local telegram service (and little point in sending telegrams to the UK, where they are only telephoned to the recipient and later delivered with the mail).

**Telex**. Your hotel may have a telex that you can use. Public telex facilities are available at St John's Square, Valletta, and at Luqa Airport, 9am-5.30pm Monday-Saturday (except holidays), and at St George's Road Main Telegraph Office at the same hours from Monday to Friday (except holidays).

**Fax**. Facsimile transmission services are available at Telemalta main offices in Valletta, Sliema, St Julian's and Victoria (Gozo). Your hotel may also offer this service.

## PUBLIC HOLIDAYS

These are the official civic and religious holidays when banks, offices and shops are closed. Not listed are the numerous *festi* on various weekends in different towns, though shops then usually remain open on Saturdays.

| | |
|---|---|
| 1 January | New Year's Day |
| 10 February | St Paul's Shipwreck |
| 19 March | St Joseph's Day |
| 31 March | Freedom Day |
| 1 May | May Day |
| 7 June | Commemoration of 7 June 1919 |
| 29 June | St Peter and St Paul |
| 15 August | Feast of the Assumption |
| 8 September | Our Lady of Victories |
| 21 September | Independence Day |
| 8 December | Immaculate Conception |
| 13 December | Republic Day |
| 25 December | Christmas Day |
| Moveable date | Good Friday |

## PUBLIC TRANSPORT (See also CAR HIRE)

**Bus services**. All towns and many villages are linked up by low-cost, regular and efficient services, though in summer the buses get rather hot and crowded. You pay your fare to the driver. In Valletta, buses for all parts of the island leave from the Triton Fountain just outside City Gate. In Victoria, Gozo, the terminal is in Main Gate Street. Destinations are indicated by numbers on the bus, and you can find out which number goes where from boards at the station, or by asking at your hotel desk, the Tourist Office, or a bus driver. Buses are pea-green (Malta) or red and light grey (Gozo).

**Taxis**. They are white, are clearly marked 'Taxi' and have red number plates. All have meters, and drivers will give you an estimate of the cost of a journey in advance. A small tip (about 10%) is expected, especially when the driver has been helpful in carrying your luggage. Cabs are readily available at the airport, as well as at main hotels, around tourist centres and at the ferry docks. Hotel receptionists will order taxis for you.

**Ferries**. Apart from a summer helicopter link, the only way to get to Gozo is by boat. Sailings between Malta and Gozo are frequent, although bad weather may interrupt the service.

One passenger/car ferry leaves each morning from Sa Maison Pier in Pietà Creek, Floriana, for the main Gozo harbour, Mġarr, a trip of 1 hour 15 minutes. It has ample space, a large, air-conditioned passenger lounge and a cafeteria.

Another car/passenger ferry service, slightly less expensive and more basic, runs from Cirkewwa in north-west Malta to Mġarr several times a day. It's only a 20-minute trip, but if you start from Valletta or the airport, you have to drive to the other end of the island first. The service operates hourly in July and August (when there are sailings during the night), and every two hours at other times of year (from 6am-10pm).

For further information telephone 603965 (Sa Maison), 471884 (Ċirkewwa), 556114 (Mġarr) or 556016 (recorded information).

On Comino, the island's sole hotel runs a regular boat service to Marfa (on Malta) and Gozo at least six times a day during the summer season; telephone 473464/473051 for further details.

In addition, travel agencies and cruise companies operate Comino cruises daily. Also in summer, fast hydrofoil services operate to Gozo from Sa Maison, Sliema and Buġibba.

**Horse-drawn cabs**. First introduced in the 1850s, the *karrozzin* or horse-drawn cab has now become simply a leisurely way of visiting Valletta, Mdina and Sliema. For a rate definitely to be negotiated in advance, you can tour the main sights of the towns for an hour or so. Pick up a cab at the Customs House or at Great Siege Square in Valletta; at St Julian's outside the Malta Hilton; in Sliema, try at the ferryboat terminus on the Promenade; and in Mdina, beside Bastion Square or Mdina Gate.

**Water-taxis**. Somewhat reminiscent of a gondola, the brightly painted *dgħajsa* (pronounced 'DIGH-sa'), or water-taxi, plies Malta's main harbours. *Dgħajjes* can be hired (at rates to be negotiated) at the Customs House in Valletta and on the waterfronts at Senglea and Vittoriosa.



## RADIO and TV

Radio Malta broadcasts on two frequencies. One of them, Radio Malta International, puts on programmes in English and Italian.

On short-wave bands, reception of the BBC World Service is clear. Voice of America programmes are also easily picked up.

Television Malta transmits about five hours of programmes in Maltese and English each evening, including both British and American features. An English news bulletin preceded by a short round-up of general information, closes the daily programme at about 10.30pm or later. Most TV sets are also tuned to receive the Italian national television networks and several Sicilian local stations.

## RELIGIOUS SERVICES

Malta is almost 100 per cent Catholic. Most services are in Maltese. For non-Maltese Roman Catholics, St Barbara Church on Republic Street, Valletta, celebrates mass in French, German and English at various times. Several other denominations also have churches in Malta; see the weekend newspapers or *What's On* guide, or check with your high commission, embassy or consulate.

# T

## TELEPHONES

Public telephone boxes, found in many streets and squares, are usually painted red, but some are built of plain local stone. Phones are either coin- or card-operated (telecards can be purchased at Tele-Malta offices) and phone booths for overseas calls are clearly marked. Information in the telephone directory is in Maltese and English. For local calls, you can usually dial direct from your hotel room or by asking the operator for a line. Some hotels allow non-guests to use their lobby phones.

Overseas calls can be dialled direct to many countries, using the prefix **00** followed by the destination code. For information, dial **194** to get the overseas telephone exchange. Hotels are authorized to add an extra charge for calls placed.

For the directory enquiry service dial **190**.

The country code for Malta when dialling from elsewhere is **356**.

## TIME DIFFERENCES

Malta uses Central European Time (GMT + 1) and in summer (31 March until the third Sunday in September) clocks are put one hour ahead (= GMT + 2). Dial 195 for a time check.

**Summer chart**:

| New York | London | **Valletta** | Johannesburg | Sydney | Auckland |
|---|---|---|---|---|---|
| 6am | 11am | **noon** | noon | 8pm | 10pm |

## TIPPING

A service charge is sometimes included in restaurant bills, but in any case it is customary to leave a small tip as well. The chart below gives some suggestions as to how much to leave.

| | |
|---|---|
| Porter, per bag | 10-20¢ |
| Hotel maid, per week | 50¢ |
| Waiter | 5-10% |
| Lavatory attendant | 10 ¢ |
| Taxi driver | 10% |
| Hairdresser/Barber | 10-15% |

## TOILETS

There are few public conveniences and these are only in the larger towns. The signs differentiating men's and women's toilets are very subtle – sometimes you have to ask. If you see an attendant, you may give him or her a few cents. 'Keep this place clean,' cautions one sign in a Valletta convenience. 'Legal action will be taken.' Cafés and bars usually have facilities you can use.

## TOURIST INFORMATION OFFICES

There is an Air Malta information desk at the airport, where they can advise about hotels and give other information.

The office to contact for detailed brochures on hotels, self-catering flats, etc is the National Tourist Organization at:

280 Republic Street, Valletta; tel. 224444/225048/238282.

There is also a tourist information office at: 1, City Gate Arcade, Valletta; tel. 237747 and others at main holiday centres, where the staff also give brochures and maps.

In Gozo, go to the Tourist Information Office at Mġarr harbour, near the ferry landing pier (tel. 557407) or in Palm Street, Victoria (tel. 556454/558106).

**Tourist organizations and information for Malta abroad**:

**Eire**: Sean Carberry Associates, 22 Ely Place, Dublin 2; tel. (01) 611044.

**United Kingdom**: Malta National Tourist Office, Suite 300, Mappin House, 4 Winsley Street, London W1N 7AR; tel. 071-323 0506.

**USA and Canada**: Maltese Consulate, 249 East 35th Street, New York, NY 10016; tel. (212) 725 2345 or:

Embassy of Malta, 2017 Connecticut Avenue NW, Washington DC 20008; tel. (0202) 462 3611/2.

## WEIGHTS AND MEASURES

For fluid and distance measures see p.113.

**Temperature**

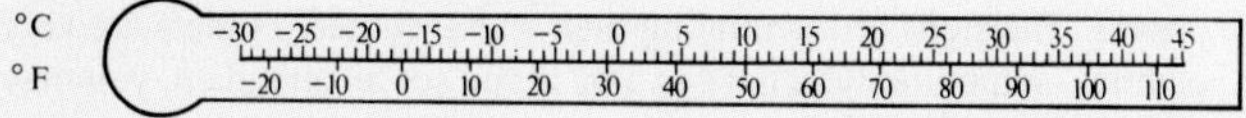


**Length**

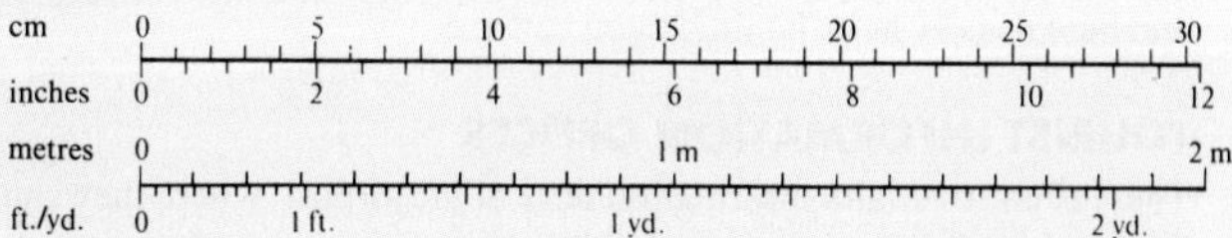


**Weight**

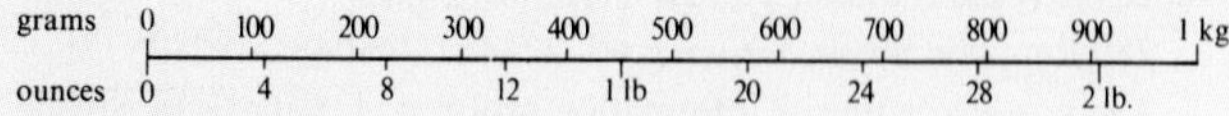

## YOUTH HOSTELS

There are several youth hostels in Malta and one in Gozo. For information, contact the Valletta Youth Hostels Association:

17 Tal-Borg Street, Paola; tel. 239361.

## Help with the menu

The list below contains a selec tion of the words (Maltese, Italian and French) that you might come across on a Maltese menu.

| | |
|---|---|
| **abbachio, agnello, agneau** | lamb |
| **aglio, ail** | garlic |
| **anitra, canard** | duck |
| **antipasto** | starter (appetizer), hors d'oeuvre |
| **bistecca** | beefsteak |
| **boeuf, manzo** | beef |
| **braġoli, bragioli** | beef olive |
| **carciofi, qaqoċċ** | artichoke |
| **ċerna** | grouper fish (*mérou*) |
| **coniglio, lapin, fenek** | rabbit |
| **dolce** | dessert |
| **espadon, pesce spada** | swordfish |
| **fagioli, fagiolini, haricots** | beans |
| **formaggio, fromage** | cheese |
| **frutta** | fruit |
| **funghi, champignons** | mushrooms |
| **gâteau, torta** | cake |
| **ġbejna** | Maltese sheep's milk |
| **homard, astice** | lobster |
| **insalata, salade** | salad |
| **lampuka** | type of dolphin-fish special to Malta |
| **melanzana** | aubergine, eggplant |
| **naranja** | orange |
| **patate, pommes de terre** | potatoes |
| **pesce, poisson** | fish |
| **piselli, petits pois** | peas |
| **prosciutto, jambon** | ham |
| **salsa** | sauce |
| **scampi, crevette** | shrimp, prawn |
| **pâtes** | pasta |
| **tonn, tonno, thon** | tuna (tunny) |
| **uove, oeufs** | eggs |
| **vongole** | clams |

# Index

Numbers in **bold** refer to the main entry listed.